Towards a Critique of Production

A Philosophical Inquiry

by

Pierre Watter

DORRANCE PUBLISHING CO., INC.
PITTSBURGH, PENNSYLVANIA 15222

ISBN # 0-8059-3631-9
Printed in the United States of America

First Printing

For information or to order additional books, please write:
Dorrance Publishing Co., Inc.
643 Smithfield Street
Pittsburgh, Pennsylvania 15222
U.S.A.

For My Wife

Acknowledgment

My thanks are due to the heirs of Antonio Machado for permission to use the quotation from *Juan de Mairena* in my translation, the copyright of which remains theirs.

It is difficult to build a new city in a waste land;
on the other part, there is material enough at
hand, but there are also all the more obstacles
of another kind, when it is desired to give a new
plan to an old city, firmly built and never without
owners and inhabitants. It is necessary to make
this resolve among others—that no use at all
shall be made of a great deal of the stock which
elsewhere is held in value.

—Hegel, *Science of Logic, II*

That two and two necessarily make four, is
an opinion many share. But if someone truly
feels differently, then let him say so....And we
may not even demand that he give proof of his
assertion, for that would be the same as to force
him to accept the rules of our thinking, on which
the arguments that might convince us would have
to be based. But these rules and these arguments
can only prove our thesis. They can in no way
prove his.

—Antonio Machado, *Juan de Mairena, I, xxx*

Contents

Foreword

This essay is the outcome of yet another failure—this one, the attempt set afoot primarily by Joseph Weber in 1947/48 with the appearance of the magazines *Dinge der Zeit* and *Contemporary Issues* to found a movement that would radically change society without, as heretofore, instituting only a new, and worse, tyranny. Rejecting Marx's political theory, Weber conceived of an organisation which would be proof against corruption and bureaucracy, against being used for ends other than those originally proposed, one that, were its endeavours not to succeed, ought, unlike conventional organisations, simply to collapse and disappear, as indeed happened. Weber himself allowed of the possibility of failure; but only of one attributable mainly to "inadequate human material," to weakness of character and intellect, in short, to factors extraneous to his concept, indeed, to the very idea of so changing society, the theoretical validity of which remained for him self-evident. This follows from his acceptance of Marx's economic theory which dismisses production as such, production as a finite teleological activity, as a generality of no particular interest. If, however, such failure be inherent in the very attempt, owing precisely to its being conceived and carried out as a purposive act subject to the irrefragable limitations of finite teleology—so that the tediously iterated conventional laments about "betrayal" would refer only to the manner in which this unavoidable result had come about—then the entire theory, economic as well as political, must fall to the ground in all its now varied manifestations. To show this to be so was at first the single burden of this work.

Examination of production as such as a finite teleological activity elucidated unsuspected connections, with the consequence that ideas about freedom, Nature, knowledge, about man and society, about history and development, and so on, came to be seen to need radical reconsideration. It became evident that, if the analysis were to be thorough, conventional notions could not be taken for granted without the risk of self-contradiction. For some of these, e.g. Nature, freedom, a critical point of departure lay to hand in the work of Kant, even if the manner in which

xi

the matter had there been dealt with was no longer wholly adequate. For others nothing was available, and it was a matter of trying to grasp and make clear what a critical standpoint, taking nothing for granted other than that productive activity is of its nature teleological, demanded with respect to them, relative to this.

The difficulty was (and is) that, especially where fundamental notions and their connections are in question, the attempt to think things afresh is bedevilled by the virtual impossibility of coming to an end of conventional determinations. The process of rethinking thus requires, to begin with, that one become aware of the mere circumstance that some idea has been taken for granted, something not always easily achieved. It is certain that instances will be found where this has not been done, and inconsequence and illogicality have resulted. This is distressing enough.

More distressing, however, is the assurance of the certain existence of errors beyond any of these that might be found, of a quite different order. These arise from some or other of the very determinations informing the knowledge and experience to which present production in the entirety of its connections, viz. society, man, and Nature, absolutely limits us; errors as unknowable to us for what they actually are, as are these determinations but for which the knowing and experiencing that we alone are, and can alone be, capable of, would be impossible. The exhibition of these, the (to me) really interesting errors, could result only from the arising of a new hypothesis, a new society, human nature and Nature, the limitations of which, being other than our own, would throw our own and the errors consequent upon them into relief—when, presumably, there would no longer be any interest in doing so.

This essay is not, in the academic sense, a scholarly work. It would be absurd to appeal to authority and acknowledge provenance where what authority has established is called into question, whomsoever and wheresoever it may come from. The attempt at something new must needs proceed in the manner of Vico, as if no books on the matter had been written, since it is the very inadequacy of the existing books that prompts to that attempt.

Such an attempt is bound to be premature and show the defects of inexperience. Yet it itself is the only road to maturity, to a proper grasp of what is involved, to experience sufficient to make good what at first was inevitably wanting. But the mind that originates is unlikely to be the one to carry the matter to its proper conclusion (namely, its replacement by a better theory), owing precisely to its being the originator, formed on conventional lines and unable wholly to transcend this limitation in other than exceptional moments of intuition, of creation.

To publish the work in, in this sense, its unfinished state is thus unavoidable, if it is to be made public at all, something I feel the matter to be of such interest as to deserve, if not, indeed, peremptorily to demand. This being so, I see no call to affect to apologise for inevitable and so far irremediable shortcomings, such as gracelessness of style, what may be thought tedious, almost rebarbative, repetitiveness, and want of order. I count them as being among the errors which, in the opinion of Voltaire, those who first quarry in new fields to some purpose must be allowed to commit with impunity.

February 1973 - June 1993

I

As concerns the relation between production and freedom, Kant and Hegel stated the basal theoretical alternatives. So powerful is the spell cast by the achievements of modern production, that Kant's view has virtually been wholly eclipsed. Even in the work of his most trenchant opponents, Hegel reigns undisturbed, frustrating critical thought at the outset. There appears to be some intrinsic equivocation in the very idea of freedom itself that makes its realisation self-contradictory, a circumstance given spurious rationality as the dialectic of freedom that at the extreme necessarily turns into its opposite, owing to either defect or excess. That this equivocation arises not from the idea of freedom but from its ground, that this ground is not proper to it—that, so far as I know, has not been seriously considered.

As a mere idea, freedom for Kant is something "the objective reality of which can in no wise be shown according to the laws of nature, and consequently not in any possible experience; (for which reason) it can never be comprehended or understood because we cannot support it by any sort of example or analogy." It is wholly different from mastered necessity which requires always submission in the shape of causality (the *modus operandi* that must be followed in order to achieve mastery), i.e., never comes about other than by the strict adherence to rule (or law), wholly beyond which rule or law freedom must lie, if it is to have a nature distinctively its own.

Aside from this seemingly wholly abstract idea, there is only the view that freedom is no other than the mentioned mastery of necessity, a mode of submission, of servitude, however qualified. This is the view of Hegel, as of Marx, which prevails. Let it be said at once that this is not wholly without substance. To be able to choose from among a number of possibilities (albeit that all, as will be shown, stringently restrict activity in definite ways, and almost always present themselves as finished products) is, for all the underlying constraints involved, better and more agreeable than being totally enslaved without any possibility of choice at all.

It might well be thought self-evident that an idea of freedom to which no content can be given that would make it rationally apprehensible and comprehensible, one defined (so far as it can be) precisely by the absence of all content of that kind, and thus apparently wholly useless, should be brushed aside as of no interest. The servitude inherent in necessity (mastered or unmastered) would then come to be accepted as an unalterable feature of human existence (a circumstance having nothing to do with happiness or unhappiness). The fact that a point of view be in present terms without any possible determinate or determinable content is, however, of itself not sufficient to warrant its rejection as an idle abstraction, since these do not exhaust the entirety of all possible terms. It may, on the contrary, be that this inability of present terms to give that point of view determinate and determinable content is a reflection of the inadequacy of these terms. This could be perceivable only to such an abstraction which thus might constitute a vantage point from which it could be inferred that the said terms have a premise (or premises) and that this (or these) must be limited, even if, for reasons to be set forth, neither the premise (or premises), nor the limits could become for us objects capable of being known and experienced for what they actually are.

If freedom be this empty abstraction, it is Nature that must be considered if the relation of mutual exclusion between them is to be made intelligible. Here again, alternatives are found in Kant and Hegel. The latter's view, that knowledge of Nature in itself is possible, once more prevails. The difficulty involved in knowing that such knowledge is possible, i.e., that Nature not known is essentially the same as Nature known, requires for its removal some assumption itself unprovable. Hegel's is the postulate of the ontological existence of Mind. Marx and Marxists have others. But the result, the deification of necessity, is the same in both, the inevitable consequence of a rationality that is only illusory.

Apart from some such assumption, there remains only one point of view, that we know, and can know, only that which we ourselves have produced, Kant's view, that knowledge of Nature "in itself" is impossible. For this view there can be a strictly rational explanation. About what is unknown, nothing can with reason be said, neither whether it be knowable or unknowable. What is conventionally called Nature was at first (and to some indefinable extent still is) such an unknown. Its determination in any way involved an act of production necessitated by the struggle for survival. This determination as whatever it might be, constituted Nature as, to that extent and in that form and with that content, known and knowable, i.e., only and exclusively in relation to the needs of the human struggle for survival. The very manner in which knowledge comes about makes absolutely unknowable to us what Nature may be out of relation to this, "in itself," for all that we must accept that it exists, in that our determination and knowledge of Nature exclusively in terms of human needs cannot self-evidently be exhaustive of all possibilities "in

2

Nature." The Nature knowable to us I call (following Cicero) second Nature, and that unknowable owing to the very production of second Nature, first Nature, distinguished from the unknown that remains (which I shall call "the original") by the circumstance that we are absolutely debarred from ever having any knowledge of it.

Whatever has been brought under control becomes thereby rational, exhibits in this form the fact of having become subject to (productive) rule. That the world is more than second Nature was, heretofore, owing to the evident limitations of production, not in question. What was in question was the security of second Nature such as it existed at any time (society and the environment that formed part of it, together with the associated human nature) in face of the unknown, something sought in the only way possible, the endowing of the unknown with the semblance of rationality in such form as at any time reason had been produced. Magic, myth, religion are, considered from the standpoint of generality, all instances of rational semblance. It is, however, clear that particular features of what in general is semblance are, for reasons here not pertinent to set out, of practical utility and thus valid as actual knowledge enabling some modicum of real control over the otherwise unknown to be exercised. Were magic, myth, religion rational semblance in all respects, the societies which to some degree depended on them for their continuance would have speedily disintegrated. That the general terms of these forms of semblance are not proper to rationality as presently conceived makes it easy to perceive that these are in fact but semblance, to perceive that they were in their general respects the manifestation of the opposite of what they ostensibly represented, inability to control in the guise of control. The modern form given to semblance, the present categorial form that (it seems to us) reason properly conceived must take, has made it more difficult to perceive, has encouraged the illusion that the semblance is what actually is, namely, not semblance at all. The most comprehensive manifestation of this form is dialectics, the representation of what, taken as a totality, is beyond knowledge and experience, as it might be supposed to be, were cognition of it possible, an illicit extension of reason that, as Kant showed, cannot but result in insoluble contradictions, restore the unknown (and unknowable) that was supposed to have been dispelled.

The prime error of Hegel (transmitted to Marx, Engels, and inheritors) lies in his rejection of Kant's unknowable thing-in-itself, in his confounding of first with second Natures, and both with the unknown original. The error points to its corrective, since the hope of freedom (in its proper signification) is vain, if the limits of rationality as presently conceived, are inherent determinations of human existence as such, and not of productive human existence merely, that of man as producer, as homo faber. Hegel's systematic dialectics, his *Logic* as the conceptual scheme of the world in motion, makes this form of rationality absolute and all-encompassing, the defining character of the world as such, not just that

3

of second Nature. Marx and Engels (as well as all Marxists) follow Hegel in this, their work constituting (whatever they may have supposed) not a critique of Hegel in this connection, but a translation of it into different terms. It is only by returning in some fashion to Kant's critical stance that a critique of Hegel and Marx becomes possible.

All men's doing, implicitly as trial and error, and explicitly as determinate and determined production, involves the formation of a Nature that is, internally and externally, theirs, a second Nature that alone has, and can have, actuality for them, something not properly grasped, so long as the formation is conceived as merely the transformation of given material; for no material is ever given with the capacity for this, i.e., never given in the form of transformable material, since nothing can be perceived as transformable except in terms of its suitability relative to a purpose that itself endows it with that capacity, which is thus already a category of production.

Second Nature is the name I give to the entirety of what men have produced, something that for them at any time exists exclusively, that they can know and experience only in the form and with the content they have themselves given it, and in terms of which they reflexively know and experience themselves in like exclusive fashion. Every society (every particular productive form of second Nature) constitutes a hypothesis about Nature and man, about the nature of Nature and the nature of man, of the correctness of which it unconsciously takes itself to be the proof, that is to say, which for it does not and cannot take the form of a mere hypothesis, but must appear to be "how things are of their very nature." This means that second Nature, Nature for man, or social productive Nature, exists and can exist only in the form of a collection of rules, both in the shape of products (of which man is himself one) and in that of their individual and concerted motions (the several ways of their production and their interrelations). Second Nature is always an abstraction. It is so on two counts: as the appropriation by means of a spontaneous creative act of a portion of the until then unknown original that the accordantly created production capacities thereupon make available (enable men not only to use, but also to perceive in a form accordant with these capacities and in such form only); and as informed into objects, endowed with such categorial form as production capacities permit, or, what is the same, classified (as Durkheim argued) in such terms as enable them to become means of production, to become subject to rule, be indeed the expression of rule(s), something always extended illicitly in some manner to what at any time does not fall into the domain of actual production. Second Nature, productive society, is intrinsically the realm of subjection, from which freedom in its correct acceptation is radically excluded, so far as whatever is in any way involved in production is concerned. So far as freedom is thought to exist in such circumstances, the appearance arises from a consciously or unconsciously willing acceptance of particular rules (for the general rule that expresses the limit of all possibilities never itself can come into consciousness, for so long as any society endures), or as the possibility of choice from among rule-determined ways of proceeding, the general limits of which (their restriction to just these) are taken as absolute, as inhering in the nature of things and man.

Hegel's resolution of the Kantian antinomies of reason by means of dialectics proves Kant's view of dialectics as a logic of illusion. It destroys reason just by making it systematic. The sentence about the real and the rational transforms the non-rational into an appearance, albeit a necessary one, indicative (*inter alia*) of a constitutive defect in man whose subjective reason can never comprehend reality. This is the reverse of Kant's view, according to which the non-rational (the unknowable thing-in-itself) is a necessary postulate of reason itself in its relation to the world, as the acknowledgment of the reality of that which man can never make objective (or actual) to himself owing precisely to the fact that his knowledge can never have other than a rational form, i.e., can be produced in no other form whatsoever. The unknowable thing-in-itself represents Kant's acceptance of the intrinsic one-sidedness of reason, for all that it is *a priori* impossible for man to know in what this one-sidedness consists, knowledge being of its nature its expression. If this be a defect, it is a defect of reason as such, not of its subjective manifestation merely. Hegel (here the true disciple of Plato) dismisses the idea of the intrinsic one-sidedness of reason, attaching one-sidedness (to keep the expression) to man's capacity for reason. The cunning of Reason that moves ever in mysterious ways makes actuality unalterably a theonomy beyond human control, and just as unalterably transforms man into a mere means constitutively unable, whatever he may fancy himself to be doing, of knowing what he really does, the actual import of his action. The progress of freedom extrinsically chartered in the *Philosophy of History* is that of the freedom of Mind (assumed to have ontological existence), and history, properly understood, is that of its self-development from immanence to actuality, the intrinsic pattern of which is set forth in the *Logic*.

Hegel's error is seen in the schema of dialectical movement presented in the *Logic*, so soon as it be inquired more clearly what it is a movement of. His criticism of what he asserts to be the inherently analytical procedures of the understanding, given in his comparison of these with the peeling of an onion, gives dialectics the higher function of reconstituting the *disjecta membra* resulting from analysis, into the interconnected whole they originally formed, restoring to them the movement, the self-movement, of which analysis by dismemberment deprived them. The conception is based on an error. To suppose that analysis dismembers is to assume the prior existence of an object, to assume, that is, that it is in itself, independently of being known, essentially what it is, as known. In reality, what Hegel sees as dismemberment is an aspect of the mode of production of an object, as that which alone we can know. But this can never be the beginning. Initially there can have been only the spontaneous creation of that which, at first more or less inchoate, by trial and error and reflection thereon (a reflection made possible only by that very original intuition and subsequent trial and error), becomes in this, the course of its becoming objective and objectified, sc. produced, the object that can be the subject of analysis. Analysis, both as procedure and in its effects, is always limited to what, and by what, has been constituted as the objective, objectified, world, has been so produced. It belongs wholly to second Nature. What Hegel considers the result of synthesis, the supposed restoration of some self-movement to an object, is in effect the mode in which constituted objects are brought into relation in accordance with some productive requirement, some productive purpose, in terms of which, as accomplished process, they then retrospectively acquire the status of analysed, or analysable, parts, something which, out of relation to that process, that purpose, they never could do. Even when analysis has become a settled mode of procedure (something that argues the prior production of an already fairly large and diverse second Nature), no object is ever, ever can be, analysed into parts other than in terms of a purpose, be it but prospective, fanciful, which itself dictates the terms in which the analysis is to be made, i.e., what is to be looked for (what the purpose has itself already made potentially objective as a supposition, the correctness of which is then to be determined solely by trial and error), so that here, too, even if at first only ideally, the parts are retrospectively constituted. Hegel's presentation of analysis as externally related to synthesis (considered as a subsequent higher activity) is an error. All analysis is an aspect of the way in which a process of synthesis, of production, takes place, and is always governed by it. If an analysis be defective, it is never because of the analytical method itself as such, as Hegel asserts, but because either the process of achieving the desired synthesis has not been correctly determined, or the desired synthesis itself is impossible of achievement, in the form first proposed, or altogether.

The idea of self-movement as actual, with respect to an object, is an illusion deriving from the ontological status given to Mind (or Matter). In actuality, movement is but the *modus operandi* of an object's production (or synthesis) expressed as a series of transformations (particular productive activities) necessary for the purpose, method in the form of settled rule that has to be followed, a result in which the purposive activity that originally yielded this can in time vanish from sight, giving the appearance of independence. In logical terms (the propriety of which must be allowed for the clarification of dialectics, if for no other), movement consists of the concatenation of categories proper to the production of any object or objects, categories which themselves are the most abstract expression of the world constituted as objective, objectified, of the produced world, second Nature, categories themselves, that is, also objective and objectified, elements of that world. Dialectics disposes of nothing but just these

6

categories, which it necessarily appropriates from what in its name is disparaged as instrumental reason. What Hegel (and others) adds to these under the name of necessity (so far as this betokens something other than a causally determined procedure as a rule that imposes itself willy-nilly with respect to the production of any object) and accident are, properly considered, not categories at all, but indications of the want of categories, of that which (be it what it may) has not been made, or cannot be made, objective—an addition that robs the categories proper of their substance by making them mere vehicles of a movement they do not themselves constitute. Dialectical movement, the movement of the totality of things (as which alone it must be taken in accord with Hegel's assertion that the system alone is the truth) is not objective movement, the itself objectified inter-relation of constituted objects, that of rule-determined production. It is but semblance, the description of what is, temporarily or permanently, beyond knowledge and experience, in terms proper only to that which has been actually produced and is in that form and content alone capable of being known and experienced. Necessity and accident such as dialectics presents them are the gods (or God) in pseudo-categorial dress. The idea of self-movement as actual is part of a complex of ideas which issues into one form or another (idealist or materialist) of the reflection theory of consciousness, the erroneous presuppositions of which have already been briefly noted. Its consequences will be considered further in what follows.

Before proceeding, some remarks about realism and truth are pertinent. In relation to what I have called "second Nature," it would be absurd to question the correctness of realism. That the reflection of what has been produced should be, within limits still to be examined, correct, can surely not be doubted. Similarly, thus, in relation to second Nature can the correctness of the reflection theory (granted it be an outcome, a result, of productive activity). This is so only in theory. It does not, of course, mean that every person's reflection of the produced world is at all times correct. The correctness of the realist standpoint is one of principle, not of invariable practice. Likewise with truth. So far as the reflection of any part of the produced world be correct, so also is it true, so far as it goes. It may even be said to be absolutely true, where there is adequate knowledge for comprehensive, error-free reflection. (This, of course, is not fixed forever: production methods may change, and with this, the object that is their end, at which time the erstwhile reflection will manifestly no longer retain its character of correctness and truthfulness.)

Just as absurd self-evidently are the realist standpoint, the notion of truth and the reflection theory of consciousness, when held in relation to "first Nature" absolutely unknowable to us. And so it is relative to the unknown original. For even if some portion of the latter should have been abstracted in a knowable form and become for us a part of second Nature, there is no way whatever in which we can establish whether there was, and is, in the unknown original, independently of our production of it in the form and content alone knowable to us, anything corresponding to this knowable object of our production. That is to say, in relation to the conventionally accepted idea of "Nature" (which has been, I hold, clearly shown to be untenable), the assertion of the possibility of realism and truth, however qualified, can never be other than dogma, from a rational standpoint without substance. This is, in short, not knowledge, but semblance.

Every act of production bespeaks (as said) abstraction. It is of its nature a simplification, and only as such is production possible at all. The simplification does not consist merely in there having been an appropriation from what was before this the unknown original. It consists as much in the manner of the appropriation, in the form in which what has been appropriated becomes an object of experience capable of being recognised. Simplification is always classification (of its nature betokening standardisation and generalisation), a productive act that gives that which is its matter not simply its form, but also its determinate (limited) content, as a specific something, as which alone it becomes capable of being cognised as an object, as objective and objectified, for man. That "Nature" (including homo faber human nature) is rational means that it has been produced. That is to say, production, which supervenes upon the initial spontaneous creation of Nature as at first inchoate second Nature (and simultaneously its inescapable accompaniment, unknowable first Nature, Nature out of relation to man, human nature out of relation to homo faber), is intrinsically classic. It is, indeed, upon this standardisation or generalisation that the very possibility of re-production depends, of production at will in accordance with the rules that codify the process of standardisation, and are themselves that standardisation in the form of the pertinent sequence of operations needed for its objective, objectified embodiment as a determined and determinate thing. The cognition of something as objective, cognition as such, that is, expresses its mode of production in summary form, as an apparently immediate result. To describe any object, to manifest knowledge of it, is always implicitly to describe how it was made, to give its nature in terms of its causality, a mode of procedure having reference exclusively to (purposive) production. Causality is an essential expression of the controlling process that produces second Nature. In having been so produced, causality itself necessarily becomes an objective, objectified element in second Nature, as a tool demanded by that process. If causality is a law of second Nature, expressing (within limits) the interdependence of cause and effect, it is so only because those have been so produced as to yield precisely that interdependence. The movement (interdependence) causality both prescribes and describes is the connection brought about among, imposed upon, objectified and thereby independent elements (elements, that is, that are what they are in virtue of having been disengaged from their context in the unknown original, whatever this may have been, and whatever it may have made them, knowledge of which this very disengagement makes impossible to us) relative to a determined and determinate end. So far as the moment of spontaneity is concerned, that whereby everything radically new initially comes about, nothing useful can be said, since the very circumstance that we must describe it (if at all) as spontaneous (*generatio aequivoca*), means that it is beyond causality as known and knowable to us, beyond the limits of knowledge and experience. All production (and, *a fortiori*, re-production) bespeaks the end of spontaneity. Just in being classic, production is inescapably conventional, the repetition of an established pattern of operations that yields a like patterned objective and objectified result.

Put differently, every act of production is a determined and determinate negation. An object posited, produced, i.e., determined in this determinate form and content, is *a priori* other than what was originally, before production took place, or production would have been superfluous. What is negated by the act of production determining something as an object, as known, is by that very act absolutely shut away from being knowable. Were we to try to know it, we could do so only in terms of that which denies us knowledge of it, an absurd contradiction. Contrary to what the reflection theory must assert, every object, i.e., everything produced, and thereby alone capable of being known and experienced, is necessarily other than whatever was in the unknown original and remains as its first Nature accompaniment. The unknowable thing-in-itself, Nature out of relation to man as homo faber, to his needs, his struggle for self-preservation, is an absolute limit imposed upon production, upon the possibility of perception, knowledge, and experience, by production itself, and by the perception, knowledge, and experience deriving from and alone associated with it. Whatever effects first Nature may yield (and it is to be presumed that it do so), real as it is, and as they are (if they are)—something we are obliged in theory to acknowledge—neither it nor they can ever be or become actual for man. We are constrained to conclude that, were these to affect second Nature—something which though not in our power to assert or deny, we may, from the circumstance of the very existence of first Nature, without impropriety suppose there to occur—there would be no possibility of our knowing or experiencing them at all, that the form and content in which we might be obliged, owing to manifest disturbances "in Nature," to make them accessible to knowledge and experience, would, in so bringing them within the compass of second Nature (the only possible manner of doing so), necessarily make them other than what they might themselves "in themselves" be. The distinction is, of course, wholly abstract and of purely theoretical interest, deriving from a view of production in accordance with which on the one hand, no society is, or ever can be, other than a hypothesis about Nature and human nature, and, on the other, is, or ever can be, conscious of itself as being so. Since to itself the Nature and human nature a society produces are as they must and can only be "in the nature of things," it follows that whatever happens must needs be taken to be, at least in principle, knowable for what it is, viz., capable of being correctly reflected in consciousness. The mistranslation of first Nature into second Nature terms just mentioned never manifests as such, and indeed never can so manifest itself, being a corollary of society as hypothesis, a circumstance that today reinforces the illusion that what is supposed Nature "in itself" is not, as it is, merely semblance, but actually so (and likewise human nature). There is thus no possibility at all of dealing adequately with such disturances "in Nature" as arise in first Nature (other than by a happy coincidence that does not at all affect the matter with respect to knowledge of it, or its possibility), which occur as a fatality never perceived to be so, however ineffective our attempts may be, since the supposition remains that, even if only in principle owing to presently defective knowledge, effective action would be possible, could we but discover in what it must consist.

Such effects are wholly different self-evidently from those unforeseen and often unforeseeable effects that arise during production and can in principle be dealt with productively, show themselves to have been the consequence of some productive misconception capable of being corrected, or of some interrelation at first overlooked or at the time incapable of being even conceived of.

If one suppose second Nature and its complementary human nature (all perception, knowledge, and experience, that is) to be intrinsically hypothetical, but in such fashion that its expression at any time, society, necessarily is taken to reflect "the nature of things"—which is what the assumption of the reality of the unknowable "thing-in-itself" entails—it follows that any hypothesis of that kind radically different from our own, either one that has before existed, or that may exist in the future, is *sui generis* beyond the limits of all possible perception, knowledge, and experience set by the prevailing hypothesis.

It is thus both the future as radically different from the present that is absolutely closed to us in virtue of the social determination of consciousness, the limitation of perception, knowledge, and experience to what society makes possible (the general form in which, for us, perception, knowledge, and experience must necessarily come to be); and the past, since the present constitutes what in social terms is the radically different from it (given that some radical social change has taken place). All theories of development in terms of the "encapsulation" of the past in the present (to use Collingwood's term) are basally in error. The presumption that the present was in any way immanent in the past is a necessary consequence not merely of the irrefragable social limits of perception, knowledge, and experience that make history an essentially circular process (something observed also, though in different form, in natural history); it is, more fundamentally the manifestation of the fact that only as such can that which we call history come to be known, take the form of apparent knowledge, become in appearance, objective and objectified for us. If the past for us remained a haphazard mass of occurrences lacking any pattern that might give it some necessary relation to us, it could never be more than just this meaningless jumble. What makes the past historical, makes it, that is, the past for us, or our past, is its ordering in terms of some principle taken to be the expression of its intrinsic necessity, of the necessity of its having developed so as to issue into the present. It is this principle as necessity that itself then determines the facts of history and their interconnections (historical development, that is), produces them, i.e. history itself, as known, as re-cognisably what it is, the result, namely, of prior cognition of what are taken to be its essential forms (something that need not be, and seldom is, present as such to the mind of a historian). Such a principle as necessity, since it is that that informs history, can never itself be historical, never belong to the past, but only to the present. History, the past made intelligible as that which alone constitutes the past to and for the present, is thus of its very nature anachronistic. This is the sense of Vico's remark that "the Greeks...describe the [whole] world within their own Greece," i.e., of his perception that men know (their) history, because they have made it. History is always the expression of present dissatisfaction, present unhappiness, present problems, the attempt to explain their genesis, to discover how (if at all) they may be dealt with. Only that ever becomes historical that can be made (however indirectly) to bear upon present preoccupations. The fact that the struggle for self-preservation has in all societies up to now been the generally determining factor is what has enabled us to present the past as essentially the record of our own genesis. The possibility is what has given rise to the illusion that the past can actually be known, be re-experienced, as what it was for itself, an illusion that is merely the social form of the reflection theory of consciousness. In reality, any sense we make of the past is our own. It does not, and cannot, bear any relation (or rather, we have no means of ever knowing whether it does, or does not, bear any relation) to what the past was in itself and for itself, to know which would involve a contradiction in terms and would furthermore (were it possible) be of no interest at all, in being the expression of problems and worries alien to us, in terms likewise alien.

That history is not an adequate explanation of the present, the continuing uncontrollability of society, despite repeated and varied attempts to understand its mechanism (how it came about), makes evident. This suggests that the production of history, as have all other productions, likewise simultaneously has an unknowable residue as its complement, one relative not to the past as such (i.e., as what it was in itself that has wholly vanished and can never be recaptured), but to the present, to that in terms of which the past is constituted. History is not merely an inadequate, but can never be other than an inadequate, explanation of society, since the very terms in which history is produced is brought within the compass of perception, knowledge, and experience, themselves presuppose what is sought, in historical fashion, to explain. The very thing that needs to be explained can never be present to social consciousness at all, being that in terms of which social consciousness as such (and *a fortiori* its particular manifestation as historical consciousness) is itself informed, its social determination that sets and itself expresses the absolute limits of all possible social knowledge and experience. It is owing to the social form of this knowledge and experience itself, to that but for which no such knowledge and experience would be at all possible, that our knowledge and experience of society, the manner in which we attempt in any way whatsoever (historical, sociological, and so on) to describe it, is incurably defective, always but a simulacrum of knowledge, namely, semblance. History, or more generally, social theory, to the production of which this very defect impels, represents the self-contradictory, self-defeating attempt to go beyond the social determination, the social limits, of all possible perception, knowledge, and experience. If society were itself correctly known and experienced; if men in essential matters determined their conditions of existence, instead of being determined by them in ways at bottom unintelligible to them; if, that is, they controlled the society they constituted by their activities, they would then be capable of knowing the past to have been radically different from the present, and by that very token would know themselves to be wholly incapable of knowing in what that difference actually consisted. They would and could have no past at all, having neither need for, nor interest in, having one, a circumstance given expression in the sentence, "a happy people has no history."

Marx's jibe that for bourgeois consciousness there was a history, but that there is one no longer is misdirected—insofar as it takes this to be a defect peculiar to this consciousness, one from which social consciousness could be freed by more correct thinking, was, indeed, according to him, freed in the form of "socialist consciousness." However legitimate such a supposition might have been at the time, subsequent events have shown that *mutato nomine, de te fabula narratur,* a practical confirmation of a theoretical error. No society can see itself as historical, but only as the result of history; it is always to itself the only instance of Hegel's "thus far has consciousness come." The attempted historical explanation of this result, of what is supposed unhistorical, shows the supposition to be false, for it represents the search for the causality of society, for that which, if known, would enable society to become what it is not, stable, under control, i.e., precisely unhistorical, so far as what lies within man's capacity is concerned. Social consciousness manifests the reverse of what it appears to be, unconsciousness (ignorance) of what gives society its character of being more and other than the sum of its parts (something that gives rise to the false presumption of its having an organic nature), of being different from, and opposed to, the individuals who compose it, a circumstance that (as will be seen) arises out of the very nature of production as purposive and, *pace* Marx, can never be wholly done away with.

General social theory, the exhibition of how society works as a whole that would make this its critique, is impossible. "Scientific socialism" is a contradiction in terms, as is every other systematic explanation. Just in being systematic, these convict themselves of one-sidedness, for what gives system its character is its exclusiveness. Nietzsche's remark that the will to system betrays a lack of integrity applies not only to the attempt, always nowadays a dogmatic assertion beyond what reason can support, but also to the material, always tailored to conformity. Marx's remark that political-economy does not recognise the existence of the unemployed applies, *mutatis mutandis*, to all general social theory, put forward as definitive in defiance of Hamlet's warning.

And yet without some general theory we cannot do, if we wish to preserve the illusion, necessary to the appearance of life as essentially rational, of not being blind victims of a process, in its present form, of its nature indeterminable to, and by, us, and so uncontrollable. Paradoxically, if it were possible to cognise how society comes to be intrinsically beyond control, to understand how this comes about and why it must be so, the knowledge would give some idea of what in principle is needed to overcome this condition, albeit that as things are this might not be able to be done. Useless as this knowledge might be in such connection, it would nonetheless have the effect of dispelling illusions about the nature and possibility of radical social change (Marx's legacy), prevent the endless dispiriting disappointments arising from misconceived attempts to that end, and relieve from wholly pointless effort—all clearly advantageous.

The arbitrary starting point of general social theory to date, so far as it concerns itself with radical change, that allows it to be worked up into a system, i.e., makes it in some fundamental respect faulty, suggests that despite appearances its informing principle (whatever it may be) remains superficial, that something basic is taken for granted that should have been investigated. I am led to suppose that this want of general social theory is something so much a part of life as to seem to be of its very nature. Modern society itself supplies this something, long since pointed to by Marx in the observation that the development of technology, social productive power, puts an end to the direct dependence of production upon human labour. It is none other than human productive labour itself, in sum, production as such. Marx himself did not develop this insight which for him remained no more than an idea of no immediate significance. Indeed, so far was he from being in a position to understand what this signified, owing to the then relatively undeveloped state of production (technology), that he considered the investigation of human productive labour, beyond the most cursory exhibition of "the simple elements of the labour process" common to all forms of production, nugatory; and this despite his assertion that freedom arises beyond necessity, an idea, properly understood, that is but a variant of Kant's view earlier noted. It is only the now in principle substantially, that is to say, to a very large extent still only potentially, achieved transference of much of the actual labour of self-preservation to internally self-directing, self-regulating, machines and the effects of this in a social setting still structured in the obsolete terms of the "nature"-imposed necessity for labour, that compels attention to be directed to human productive labour, to production as such, in the hope that this may more adequately explain the circumstance that the more freedom comes to be in principle possible of achievement (or so it seems), the more impossible does it seem to become in actuality. What society manifests is but Kant's cognition that freedom and rule-guided activity (to put the matter summarily) are mutually exclusive, while showing that this in principle is no longer, and in practice need no longer be, as it inevitably was for Kant, an unalterable fatality, i.e., that the struggle for survival no longer need require that the whole of life be subordinated to its imperatives in one form or another.

II

For Marx, the specifically human character of labour is that it is purposive (a restriction that will not be quarrelled with here, erroneous though it be). Human production (to keep to this here) falls wholly into the sphere of finite teleology, and of its nature transforms man, *qua* producer, into an instrument of production under the sway of the telos that (qualifications granted) determines the entire nature and sequence of operations in terms of which alone it becomes capable of realisation. This (granted the same qualifications) holds also for the material which comes to be determined as material for production in terms of the requirements of the telos, and is material for it only in respect of those aspects of it that the telos elucidates in relation to itself (whatever else the material may be in itself being irrelevant). The determination of what a purposed production requires from both man and material, what its rules are, is always a matter of trial and error, the process whereby everything not pertinent to man in his capacity of producer specifically of the things in question, and to the matter as material for it, is eliminated. Trial and error are not themselves production, but the striving to it which, once achieved in the form of settled rule, definitive *modus operandi*, shows them to have been activity lacking the guidance of rules, inchoate activity, precisely what production rules out. Production does not merely constitute the world (Nature, society, and man); it constitutes it exclusively in the form and with the content appropriate to itself, as not just the result of activity under the guidance of rules, but as the expression of these rules, called here second Nature and homo faber.

In terms of the distinction he makes between this labour and what he calls "those first instinctive forms of labour which remain on the animal level" (a distinction wholly without substance), Marx supposes that "the land...in its original state in which it supplies man with necessaries or means of subsistence ready to hand is available without any effort on his part as the universal material for labour;" and that "all those things which labour merely separates from immediate connection with their environment are objects of labour spontaneously provided by nature, such as fish caught and separated from their natural element, namely, water, timber felled in virgin forests, and ores extracted from their veins." This supposition rests on the reflection theory of consciousness, in terms of which alone can it be supposed that man, primitively, was able, so to say, simply to help himself from "Nature's larder," i.e., that primitive man perceived what was there as it actually was, in which form it was given him by Nature itself, together with the knowledge that this was what he needed and wanted. This is the source of the mystification that attaches to what is known as reification and alienation (abstraction and objectification) considered, as it must be on such a view of consciousness, as brought about by commodity production and peculiar to it, (Marx's contention); something that makes the future appear in some fashion a return to an uncomplicated primal condition, when things were as they seemed. But this, alas, is all a fantasy, the fantasy of the loss of innocence and its recovery.

Yet, even though Marx's discussion of reification and alienation fails to reveal their source, he nonetheless is correct in pointing to these as fundamental features of present society, which we must account for if we are to grasp the import of technology, what it actually represents. We must, that is, account both for their existence as such, and for the fact that they manifest themselves in present society in a somewhat different manner from that they have previously.

Since (as already argued) the past as intelligible is but a surmise to explain present necessity (however cognised) in terms of which it is produced to that end, and since all existing such surmises fail to do so adequately, I am at liberty to propose something different that may be more fruitful.

That man was originally simply a food gatherer is Marx's supposition. But what is the gathering of "food" which, contrary to what Marx believes, cannot, as already said, be given man "by Nature." Man must find it in "Nature" and can do so only by a process of discrimination which he must himself carry out. Gathering material indiscriminately, precisely just "at the hand of Nature," is one thing. Gathering "food," material that has been subjected to discrimination from among the manifold surrounding materials with that end in view, is wholly different. "Food," as a discrimination, is something that could initially have been nothing but the spontaneous arising of an idea, the idea of the possibility of there being such a thing. This possibility could have been given actuality (if at all) only as a more or less lengthy process of trial and error, random experiment. Its achievement showed itself in the fact of its being capable of being reproduced at will, the hallmark of production as *sui generis* a conscious purposive activity (irrespective of whether altered circumstances later make this specific productive activity impossible, owing to change in climate, flora or fauna, loss of knowledge, etc.).

In sum, "food" is a production category. To denominate some material as "food" signifies that it has been identified (discriminated from other material) in respect of its capacities relative to this purpose, that it has been abstracted from among the rest and that it is only as this abstraction, as given the (even if only implicit) conceptual form of "food," that it now becomes an object of, and for, perception, comes to be perceived at all, becomes, that is, capable of re-cognition in the exclusive form and with the exclusive content in which it now exists as a produced object. "Food" gathering is the beginning of the constitution of second Nature and homo faber, of Nature and man as objective, objectified. There is, *pace* Marx, no such thing as merely separating from immediate connection with the environment, since the very possibility of such separation pre-supposes discrimination, activity in terms of a purpose not lying in the material itself, but imposed upon it as that by means of which the material comes to be perceived in just this fashion, as endowed with the capacity of being separated in the required manner. There are no "objects of labour spontaneously provided by Nature." The very idea begs the question, since before something can be an object of labour, it must first have been constituted as objective for it. Catching fish, felling timber, extracting ores argues the prior production of fish, timber, ores, categories not given "in Nature," any more than the activities of fishing, felling, and extracting, i.e., the capacities involved by these. In all, the conception of "Nature" as in any sense material "ready to hand" is thoroughly anachronistic. Because we cannot know "Nature" as other than it has been produced, as other than second Nature (and likewise "human nature" as produced homo faber nature), we readily fall into the error of assuming that what we know is the (unknown) original, mistakenly thought of as "Nature" (including "human nature"), and ascribe to them what belongs to the only Nature and human nature we can at all know, the ones we have ourselves produced, second Nature and homo faber nature. How difficult it is to keep the distinction (without which understanding of modern society is impossible), is shown by Marx in this very passage, which does not square with his view of Nature (for us) as a social product, namely, second Nature.

The exhibition of "food" as a production category is a nodal point. "Food" is not simply material in produced conceptual form (however at first merely implicit); it is as much the concept "food" in material dress, existing as a concept made objective, independently of man. This is the mode in which second Nature comes about, the source of its rationality. All produced capacities, whether of man or material, capacities that become such only in having been so produced, are by that very fact abstractions and objectifications. Their very production, that which makes them what they are (but for which they would not exist at all), inescapably involves reification and alienation, the only forms in which they can be constituted, in which second Nature, that includes homo faber, can be, and has been, constituted. In sum, one of the very first tools of production is conception, or more generally, understanding, the categories of which are production categories in their most abstract form. Objective idealism and dialectical materialism are but general modes of reflection upon production as a whole, out of which they arise, modes which would not be possible had not second Nature and homo faber been antecedently produced. Their essential shortcoming is that they take their point of departure, in the one instance the final cause, in the other the material cause, as given "in the nature of things"; whereas in effect these are features of the single (circular) process of finite teleology, which explains why the viewpoints are complementary and, each pursued to its end, merge with each other. Marx's idea (1844) of a "naturalism" that would be the truth of both reproduces the error, supposing the partiality of the several standpoints to be so in relation to "Nature," which they would fully reflect, once corrected. But the partiality is intrinsic and is not overcome by being transferred from one to the other of these standpoints, a process which merely reproduces it each time in different form, since reason is wholly enclosed in second Nature which is its expression. In terms of the perception of the unbreakable circularity of second Nature as rational production, as the production of rationality, such attempted philosophical explanations, that *sui generis* place their starting point outside a for them uncognised second Nature, become irrelevant, because self-contradictory. Their very dialectical form, to which their desired comprehensiveness impels them, betrays their want of explanatory capacity, since it arises from an unrecognised failure of understanding. From this subjective idealism (in Kant) is, for all its present-day inadequacy, exempt, precisely because its starting point is the cognition of rationality as intrinsic only to second Nature.

The fundamental category of both objective idealism and dialectical materialism, motion, which they severally grapple with, exhibits their central error, whether it be self-moving Mind, or self-moving Matter. Mind and Matter, as objects, as objective and objectified, are production categories. That Mind is so is clear from its conception as always (in this form) fashioned after the model of the final cause in finite teleology. Matter, however, seems to escape this encirclement. It seems proper to suppose that, for all that it is an abstraction, therefore a category, it nonetheless refers in its lack of definition to the "stuff" (so to say) of the unknown original. But this is an error. To call this "stuff" (whatever it may be), "matter" is to introduce a distinction without warrant, since "matter" (however indeterminate), if it is to have any sense at all, must be a negative determination. Logically, the "stuff," if it is to be all there is (the assertion of materialism), must then be more than just matter. The very terms in which we attempt to make what this may be that we try to define fall within the scope of definition, of knowledge, show the attempt to degenerate into an infinite regress. In short, matter can be nothing but the general name for whatever material has been produced, a general category of production. What has not been produced is neither mind nor matter (or at least we have no means whatsoever of ever knowing wheth-er it be either or both or neither), is, for us, nothing at all relative to the only way in which we can come to know anything. This is, of course, not to deny its reality, whatever this may be, but only to acknowledge that we are absolutely debarred from ever knowing, ever experiencing, it in the only terms available to us, proper to the activity of knowing and experi-encing. For us, mind and matter are simply the names of the most comprehensive abstractions in terms of which all produced objects can be severally classified, however difficult and questionable such classifica-tion may be in specific instances.

The definition of matter as self-moving central to dialectical material-ism, or of Mind as self-moving central to objective idealism, betokens the reverse of what they claim, the alteration of whatever motion the un-known original may have had (supposing it to have had any—a supposi-tion without any possible content, self-evidently); for what gives them this seeming independence of motion is just their constitution as that from which (so long as this constitution has not been cognised as having been produced) deduction of features appears to be able to take place, as if they were what they are independently of having been made so. Motion is part of the controlled process of production of second Nature, the substance of what are called the laws of Nature, the most general expres-sion of causality, as which alone they are properly laws at all. The fact that these laws are nothing but codified modes of productive procedure shows how vain must be their dogmatic assertion. The only verification such laws are capable of as second Nature procedures that *a priori* cannot be measured against anything outside of them as a standard, is that they work, a circumstance that can never give them the necessity such proof, advanced as theory, claims. Laws of nature are interim reports on the stage the development of production has reached. It cannot even be supposed that they are asymptotic approximations to "truth," since to do so would be to lapse into the error of the reflection theory, to invoke as a standard both the unknown original and the, to us, absolutely unknow-able first Nature as if they were not merely knowable, but known. This holds good also for homo faber, the produced nature of man, man's productive nature, or nature *qua* producer. Everything written about the "human essence," or in terms of what is taken to be "innate" to man as such, is wholly without substance, always either the unwarranted (and unwarrantable) idealisation of some existing feature, or its equally unwar-ranted (and unwarrantable) dogmatic assertion *sub specie aeternitatis*, beyond the possibility of proof or disproof.

Laws of Nature and human nature hold good only for the productive society that has so determined them. They are the terms in which a society's hypothesis about its nature and the nature of its environment, as well as that of man, about the world as it has produced it, that is, is for-mulated. There are as many such laws as there are different kinds of productive societies, each of which constitutes an absolutely exhaustive hypothesis about itself and Nature, of the correctness of which it unconsciously takes itself to be the proof. Magical procedures are as much expressions of laws of Nature and human nature, as are our own. That we term them magic, distinguish them in this way from what we determine to be science, means only that we have a different hypothesis from that which gave them their productive warrant. The classification does not constitute a disproof of their validity which relates to a world wholly unintelligible to us, as is shown by our inability to explain to ourselves in the rational terms peculiar to our own hypothetical world, such occurrences as come within our ken, which we encounter (but cannot bring within the compass of our experience) in societies we call primitive, i.e., consider, in the light of the history we produce as the record of our own development, to be imperfect prior attempts to be what has been realised only in our own society. The acknowledgment, as by Levi-Strauss, of the prejudicial nature of this classification alters nothing. All previous societies are in some degree, in some respect, primitive for us, or they are nothing that we can (or could) at all picture to ourselves. The description of totem and taboo (laws of nature, society, and human nature), for instance, constructs them in such a way as to enable us to understand the functions we presume them to have had, but cannot inform us of what they were as actually experienced and known. Our very imagination, sometimes supposed to be able to do what reason in this connection cannot do, is limited to what our world permits and never tells us (or can tell us) anything but what things were like, had they been as we can imagine them, irrationally as this may be done (for irrationality is itself a rational category and wholly peculiar to any particular rationality as this has been produced), i.e., reconstructs what is imagined in the terms it was intended thereby to set aside. Extinct laws of Nature and human nature are irrecoverably beyond knowledge and experience as they were "in themselves." Non-rational to us, they were not without their own reason, different from our own. The causality they expressed in the form of productive processes was effective within the world they informed, else self-preservation (for so long as this was achieved) would have been impossible. But the self so preserved was radically different from our own, as was the world, the preservation of which, in terms of their quite other capacities and needs, required wholly different means. To experience that world we should have to be other than ourselves, a condition that underscores the absolute impossibility of our ever being able to do so.

Some comments are appropriate here. They will amplify what was earlier written about the relation of science as conventionally known and accepted, and semblance (as, for example, magic). What informs the belief that science, considered in terms of its principles, wholly excludes semblance, is the supposition that it can and does reflect "Nature" and reproduce it as it actually is "in itself," even if in somewhat simplified form;

and resulting from this, that the mastery of "Nature" so conceived through the instrumentality of science is, at least in theory, in principle, possible, it being a matter largely of adequate knowledge.

But if, as has been argued, the reflection of "Nature" as it is "in itself" is an impossibility, since we are absolutely debarred from having any knowledge that would allow us to do so, science, with reference to this supposed reflection and consequent mastery, becomes nothing but semblance, and is, in this respect, no different from magic.

To digress a moment here: The so-called "laws" of dialectics are quite different from these. Whether as the transformation of quantity into quality (or vice versa), or as the interpenetration of opposites (or whatever else it might be), they are either the illusorily rational expression of what is for us beyond knowledge and experience; or they are needless additional general descriptions of what has been produced and has been brought within the compass of knowledge and experience as a causally determined and determinable specific something. As general assertions (other than which they cannot be), they are, contrary to what Engels asserted, of no practical value whatsoever.

As before said, the very survival of man from the beginning required tools, of which the first were his body and mind, always, of course, related in some way to some aspect of the environment (at first presenting itself as the unknown original, portions of which are later productively transformed into second and first Natures at the same time as the related portions of mind and body are transformed into homo faber nature). It is easy to assume capacities in mind and body, and in "Nature," to have existed potentially and to explain their emergence as but an actualisation. But this is a mistake. The practice of retrospection involved here is so ingrained, that the fact that it occurs scarcely obtrudes itself upon consciousness. Yet the perspective of a radically new phenomenon that it gives, as seen from the vantage point of its completion or result, wholly changes its nature, causing it to appear as if it had been in principle known and knowable from the start, so that its first inchoate expression merely elucidated this in practice. Such a perspective, however, robs the phenomenon of its character of being radically new, of being unknown and unknowable up to the point of its suddenly erupting into being in spontaneous, unforeseeable, and inexplicable manner.

To stress the point, what seems to have been, looking backwards, is not at all, and cannot at all be, what actually took place looking forwards, for here there is, and could be, no perspective of this kind at all.

It cannot sufficiently be emphasized that the radically new, if it is to be so, and no mere variation of something in some way already existing, can do no other than spring up spontaneously, be created (for us) *ex nihilo*.

Faced by this in basal respects unsatisfactory situation, which denies the very possibility of a causal explanation that would exhibit it as a comprehensively knowable process, it is tempting to resort to ideas such as potentiality, propensity, probability, instinct, genetic predisposition, and so on, all, in their several ways, forms or modes of essence. But what results from the use of these, however rational in appearance and seemingly reasonable, can be nothing but semblance. For no explanation of any kind (not one merely owing to the state of present knowledge) affects the circumstance that we remain, and must remain, completely and unalterably ignorant about the causality of spontaneous creation, of the emergence of the radically new (for us necessarily and forever arisen out of nothing). Retrospective explanation from the vantage point of completion must needs be at bottom determinist and mechanical. This gives a false picture by involving necessity in a manner that cannot actually have come to be. If one wishes to bring in necessity at all, then, considering the matter prospectively, it is the choice of one possibility among others that brings about the necessity of the procedure attributable to it. In general, then, putting the progression schematically, it is these successive choices that produce the several different necessities involved by the possibilities disclosing themselves at every nodal step. Whereas with the recourse to essence in any form, it is one single necessity that must be assumed to have shaped and determined a development from start to finish.

Reconstituting the process as it actually took place is impossible. There is no way at all of bringing back to life the clusters of possibilities from which a choice had to be made, every time it was a question of deciding what was the correct way to proceed. Looking backwards, what we produce as perceptible and intelligible is inevitably a simplification that gives a false appearance of more or less straightforward progress. And it is this false appearance that incites to the belief in an encompassing single necessity determining a process from start to end and so producing it as a development.

To put the matter strikingly: Looking forwards, and giving its crucial importance to choice, the factors deciding which must remain unknown, if not unknowable (so that it is not straining matters to consider choice as a form of accident), there is no way of producing a process as an intelligible progression other than in the most schematic manner that tells one virtually nothing substantial about any specific process and its actual progression.

Retrospectively, a specific process can be produced as an intelligible progression. But for reasons sufficiently clear not to need labouring here, what results can be but semblance, not knowledge.

The use of ideas moreover, of whatever kind they may be, that imply the actualisation of a potentiality, has a tendency to diminish awareness and so appreciation of the toil, the struggle, the disappointments and failures, the production of new capacities (whether of man or material, most often of both simultaneously) inevitably involves; as of the strength of character, in any of its many manifestations, needed to accomplish what has been begun, always without any possible prior knowledge, let alone experience, of what demands this will make. Looking forwards, to repeat, there is no pre-existing thread (other than perhaps exceptionally) to be discerned that points the way and thus constrains to this act rather than to that. Step by step, everything has to be decided upon. And at every step what confronts man is a cluster of possibilities from among which a choice has to be made, the correctness of which has every time to be established by trial and error. Of this labour no trace remains in the result. How many false starts were made, how many of the given possibilities were explored—of this nothing is revealed to posterity (other than, once more exceptionally, when for example, a written record has been kept), for which consequently the whole process gives the impression of having taken place almost automatically, one thing leading necessarily to the other, a circumstance once more predisposing to acceptance of some determinist point of view.

To digress for a moment: It is probably correct to assert that, in principle, spontaneity is necessary. But that cannot tell us anything about its generation, about the time, place, and conditions of its manifestations; nor about the productive transformation of what has so arisen into something apt for use at will. For there is no necessity that the subjective requirements for this should be present. Indeed, who can say how many spontaneous creations have come to nothing, for want of the needed conditions to turn them to use?

Looking forwards, what happens is, as argued, the sudden spontaneous occurrence of a radically new act or idea (whichever being first suggesting its possible other) in response to a need of the struggle for survival. This, associated with the corresponding aspect of the environment (the perception of which is itself not necessarily given or immediate), brings some heretofore non-existent capacity of both into being, or is itself that capacity *in posse*. At first the strange act or idea or capacity can but, almost always, have an unavoidably crude form and substance, apt neither for correct conception or use. Trial and error, experiment with idea, act, and environment, their several mutual corrections (and no other way is possible, a process during which memory simultaneously arises as a capacity), gradually refine them, until at length (if all should have answered), idea, act, and environment acquire the settled form and content that allows of their most advantageous and easy use at will. At this point, mind, body (the constitution so far of homo faber), and environment (become so far second Nature) can be said to possess the capacity, or capacities, in question.

I find it difficult to believe that productive activity of this kind that gives mind and body some new form and content should not be accompanied by some related biological change, however small. The production of new capacities, whether of mind or body, or subsequently also as implements that enlarge physical and mental capabilities (and give them clear independent existence), signifies the production, within their compass, of a new human nature concomitantly with the related production of the accordant portion of the environment as second Nature, and by this very circumstance, in principle or in fact, alters social relations correspondingly. If the first suggestion be correct, it becomes possible to suppose that social relations have a connected biological foundation. And thus, that societies radically different from one another in any way, have accompanying differences in their biological foundations which, slight as they may be, have yet a considerable significance. But for this, social change would inescapably have to be looked upon as but an extended masquerade in which the identical actors ("man" in general) merely donned a variety of costumes and masks that had no constitutive effect upon them, an absurd instance of the mentioned historical anachronism seen to advantage in Hollywood "historical" films.

But capacities, mental or physical, are not perdurable, any more than are those of second Nature. They can and do decay and disappear, namely, cease to be produced, when circumstances make their production no longer relevant or possible. That is to say, to the extent that this occurs, to that extent do the second Nature and associated homo faber nature cease to be produced, decay, and disappear, to be replaced by new and different ones, newly created and produced with newly created and produced capacities. And thus it comes about that it becomes impossible to re-experience anything in the past that is radically different from what currently exists. Radical new learning requires and is complemented by radical unlearning in organic as in social respects, and the former is impossible without the latter. Marx's words, "all mythology masters and dominates and shapes the forces of nature in and through the imagination; hence it disappears as soon as man gains mastery over the forces of Nature. What becomes of the Goddess Fame side by side with Printing House Square?" must be taken to refer not merely to mythology, but also to the capacity for it, to a mode of perception, cognition, and experience that we no longer have. It is but shallow thinking that can suppose that mode, that capacity, to remain in a state of suspension, that new capacities, new modes of perception, cognition, and experience (with their associated organic changes) can come about and lie side by side with the old they displace in "man," like so many different kinds of tins in a box. The difference between mythology as it was and any present-day mythologising is aptly summed up in the remark, "in the Middle Ages men built cathedrals; now they build Gothic cathedrals." The reproduction of past social artifacts in radically different social conditions (with all that this involves with respect to human capacities) is always in terms of altered capacities, altered perceptions, knowledge, and experience, i.e., always in essential respects different from the original, a mere simulacrum. These can, that is, never be "faithful" to the original, identical with it. Witness, for example, present-day "authentic" performances of early music

24

which, even though original instruments may be used, cannot sound as it did in its own day, when it was without the presently unavoidable context of comparative aural experience and knowledge.

The same is so of texts, no matter how scrupulously edited with the most conscientious scholarship, howsoever formally identical with their originals they may be. For, given the disappearance of previous second Natures and accordant homo faber natures, and the present existence of, in some important respects, different ones, the very language in which these were written is, as a living reality, completely foreign to us who no longer have the contemporary perceptions, knowledge, and experience needed to grasp and understand it as it was by those who did have them. The allusions and associations arising out of actual life, the emotional resonances that gave earlier languages their actual full sense and complexities have gone and can never be recaptured. If we wish at all to read texts belonging to former, radically different societies, try as we may to avoid this (assuming awareness of these barriers to be there at all), we necessarily do so as abstractions, which we unavoidably inform in terms of our own perceptions, knowledge, experience, associations, and resonances. What is so produced is self-evidently not the original. And we have no means whatsoever of ever knowing whether what we know in this, the only fashion in which we can do so, bears any relation at all, and if so what relation, to what extent, and in what respect, to that which it was for contemporaries, since to do so would require that we have their perceptions and so on, something absolutely impossible.

In the sphere of finite teleology (into which tools *qua* production fall) every tool (and this includes human capacities as tools) is the manifestation of reification (abstraction) and alienation (objectification), within its limits which always include that to which the tool is applied, a portion of the environment itself also becomes a tool, and by a reverse movement (so to say), becomes "subjectivised," part now of homo faber nature, as perceived, known, and experienced as a tool. Every tool is a produced capacity not merely in the sense of being the creation (and subsequent production and re-production) of that capacity in man and environment; but also in the sense of being a product existing (at least potentially in the case of many capacities of man and environment initially) either independently of, or (if it be some portion of the environment as a tool), within man. Every tool is thus in its use a produced capacity of the environment which it is the means of appropriating, of producing in relation exclusively to human needs, thus necessarily one-sidedly, without regard for what the intrinsic need(s) of what has been so appropriated may be. In finite teleology, reification and alienation always involve subjection (which, in man at least, is one of the ways in which subjectivity comes to be experienced, as an expression of suffering). Tools are not external adjuncts of man, but essential features of him as producer, homo faber. More than the style, the tool is the man (as, that is, homo faber strictly, something never to be lost sight of). Similarly in the context of finite teleology, the environment (the material cause) forms part of the stock of tools, as manipulable elements subserving production, themselves created, produced, and re-produced to that end, and, from the standpoint of production, of man *qua* homo faber, exhaustively exhausted in that relation. Finite teleology acknowledges the reality only of what falls within its scope, only of what can be abstracted, reified, objectified, alienated as part of its processes, whether man or Nature. This is not a defect, but (as earlier said) the very condition but for which production could not take place at all. It is in this sense that we must understand Marx's description of industry (including the environment it produces as a part of itself) as "the open revelation of human faculties," given that these are homo faber faculties, which are not all there is to man.

Every tool is, in the first instance, a spontaneous creation, and only as such is it the manifestation of the arising of some new capacity. Its first appearance as something new can result only from spontaneous imagination, the unexpected, unforseeable outcome perhaps of a prior series of attempts at solving some problem existing tools have given rise to but do not seem able to solve; or, at the very beginning of production, at solving some problem for which no tools (i.e., no capacities) exist at all. The tool, once so imagined in some fashion, can be produced, can become an object; or, what is the same, what has merely been imagined can be made objective as an idea, an object of, and for, cognition, the ideal tool capable in principle of being grasped in terms of its specific inherent necessity, which is always a reflection, never as such original. Cognition is of its nature objective. The only way in which it comes to be definitively itself is via re-cognition, as having been, in whatever manner this may be, objectified, first produced as an independently existing thing. Properly grasped, to think is always to be being thought. Reification and alienation, abstraction and objectification, however these may be called, are intrinsic to reason, the essential form of its constitution. The inversion whereby what man does appears done to him, which Marx wrongly attributed to the mechanism of commodity production only (the "fetishism of commodities"), is in reality no appearance, but the way in which production actually takes place, and can only take place. Purposive production (a pleonasm, since only what has been purposed can, strictly speaking, be said to have been produced) imposes its necessity in the very purpose that it is intended to achieve. Contrary to what seems to be reasonable, it is the supposition that, since the purpose is a man's own, it is under his direction, that is the appearance, the illusion. The purpose becomes properly what it is, only so far as it is understood in its own terms, not as a man may think it, but as it has to be thought, whatever may at first have been fancied. So understood, and so only, as independently existing, as other than man's capricious imaginings, does it become objective, rational for him, in the only form in which this can be, as that which determines and directs his activities, i.e., makes them rational relative to that end (and only that is rational that achieves this), an alien power that uses him to realise its own purpose, one that he must accept as his in place of that which he had before imagined. The flow is not, of course, wholly one-directional. Material, efficient, and perhaps even formal cause can oppose a resistance which may compel some change in the final cause. But the final cause remains dominant. To master anything is always in the end to be mastered by it. It is not because man is rational that the world is rational (so far as it is so); it is because he can produce the world in no other way than as rational that he becomes rational, and he does so only insofar as he is a producer, only in his function of homo faber. Reason is not merely reflective, but, with respect to man (to restrict myself to him here), wholly reflexive. It is only in terms of the idea, the necessity, that the produced tool can be refined, made to approximate to what it ought ideally to be. At the inception of human production of second Nature and homo faber, such an idea is not, as it later becomes, a mere addition to the stock of ideas. It is the creation of the very capacity for cognition, and of the perception, the perceptive mechanism, that accords with it, the creation of a new world that *eo ipso* takes the shape of production, or social, relations with respect both to man and material. A tool is a new way of perceiving (and conceiving of) whatever it relates to, and whatever relates to it, the fashioning of a new world at its level, within its capacities, or what is the same, within the capacities of man and material as they have now been produced. And what is perceived in novel fashion must antecedently have been in some fashion cognised in novel fashion. Every productive development supervening upon a new spontaneous creation is a development not just of the specific capacity that that creation has brought about, but also of the reflective capacity associated with it.

A tool is intrinsically also a means of communication with the environment which, from its standpoint, includes man so far as he is its agent, uses it as it must be used, something he learns, to which he disciplines himself as part of the subordination he forcibly undergoes in the course of production. So far as a tool alters the environment, produces it as the manifestation of some newly created form and content, to that extent does it compel the several parts of the environment to communicate with one another in the required altered fashion which, with respect to man, brings about an alteration in receptivity in order that it may be understood, brings about the needed change in cognition and perception, i.e., produces the cognition and perception it had implicitly brought about in virtue of what is it and does. Vygotsky's suggestion that conceptual language is a marriage of earlier forms of communication that comes about at some stage owing to the activity of self-preservation (production), is most fruitful. His investigations into their relations, their interconnections, led him to the conclusion that, so far as concerns the proper realisation of concepts, absolute correctness occurs not in natural language, but in mathematics only.

A remark of Hegel's is pertinent here. Nature [he writes] "is impotent to adhere strictly to thought-determinations in their purity." The curious form that derives from his assumption of the ontology of Mind, does not invalidate the insight, which may be understood thus: At a certain point in its creation and re-production in causally abstract or, what is the same, conceptual form, second Nature experiences a check owing to the inherent limit to the possible "purity" of the capacities of homo faber, until then adequate to the purposes of production. The reification of these capacities, and their alienation, the form in which production comes about, can never result in that degree of realisation of their ideal nature second Nature then requires for its further development, so long as homo faber remains their vehicle. It is, however, only the fact that these capacities already exist as independent objects, in objective and objectified manner, that permits them to be cognised in the terms proper to their intrinsic necessity, that could up to this point be only imperfectly grasped, owing to their remaining, even in objective, objectified form, the capacities of homo faber. Subsequently, their development, in becoming what it ought ideally to be (or at least a nearer approximation to this), exhibits increasingly the incapacity of homo faber relative to this. The error of Marx concerning reification and alienation is strikingly illustrated in his description of this as follows: "in bourgeois economics—and in the epoch of production to which this corresponds—this complete working out of the human content appears as a complete emptying out, this universal objectification as total alienation." Commodity production itself is not the source of this result, but a means of bringing to new heights what lies in the nature of production itself. Nor does this result signify the complete working out of the human content, that of homo faber; but the working out of what is beyond this content. But for this, the severance of the direct dependence of production upon human labour would be impossible. It is only because homo faber becomes relatively superfluous with respect to production that the possibility arises of man's being able in some measure to stand aside from it (and from himself as homo faber) and consider it as a whole. This perspective is a *sine qua non* for its control, only because, as the manifestation of the actuality of capacities wholly beyond those of homo faber, and now become essential to it, production is no longer dependent upon his exercise of these capacities. Control (so far as it can be exercised, something never complete, as will become evident) comes in principle to be seen to be little more than the determination of the quantum and nature of production required. Upon what grounds such a determination comes to be made does not, of course, fall within the compass of theory.

Considered from the standpoint of abstraction and objectification, second Nature, as already so far realised in modern technology, becomes literally what Schelling mistakenly supposed "Nature" (in itself) to be, "petrified intelligence." Hegel, writing of the produced world (properly of second Nature as here understood), that in it Mind is at home in that whatever it finds in it, it recognises to be only itself, was correct, foreshadowing the actuality that is coming to pass with the development of modern technology far more insightfully than Marx in this respect. The coming-to-be of second Nature in something nearer to its intrinsically adequate form, as the expression of what were initially the capacities of homo faber in a "pure form" that goes far beyond them, does not merely make these "impure" capacities redundant. Their uselessness relative to production brings about their gradual atrophy today, in the same way as we surmise this to have happened with regard to capacities inferentially assumed to have once existed but no longer to be met with. The remark of an American general reported by Jungk, to the effect that, measured by the tasks of space technology, man is a faulty construction, applies, *mutatis mutandis*, to modern technology as a whole, actually or potentially. In this man (homo faber) is not alone; merely another organism found wanting. Modern technology, that is to say, the production and re-production of new capacities originally spontaneously conceived, of necessity remodels the second Nature it inherited, in conformity with its own productive requirements, to produce a second Nature from which homo faber is increasingly excluded, owing (as said) to the very demands of production itself. This is so precisely in virtue of what distinguishes these new capacities from those of homo faber, their thoroughgoing rationality. It is this nonhuman content that oppresses man as homo faber today to a degree hitherto impossible, as it does other organic creatures whose second nature retransformation (so far as this is relevant) necessarily represents, inter alia, a renewed attempt radically to suppress their remaining areas of spontaneity in order to bring them into conformity with its productive requirements in their abstract "purity."

The harking back to the past as to a time when "man" was (supposedly) a more substantial, richer being, more "essentially" himself, had features which a better future would restore to him, as by Marcuse and others, is an error. If modern homo faber is empty compared with his earlier manifestations, it is owing to the fact that he exhibits the achievement of what in them was incomplete. Their apparent substance, that is, derives from the incompleteness of second Nature and homo faber nature, and relates wholly to the struggle for existence; his lack of it arises from the greater completeness of second Nature that not only makes this substance, the capacities of homo faber, largely superfluous, but holds out the promise (or, more correctly, the possibility) of there coming to be a life for man at least in part beyond the imperatives of the struggle for existence. What Marcuse and others of like mind deplore actually constitutes a development of, possibly, almost unimaginable hopefulness.

What is at work here is an instance of the essentialist fallacy, here with respect to "man". The concept of essence, a mode of immanence earlier mentioned, denies *generatio aequivoca*. It turns creation into development, explication, gives it historical form as the revelation of the necessity of the result, in the manner of potentiality, etc., earlier discussed. It is something to which reason is impelled in any attempt to grasp as a whole a process the causality of which escapes, or is beyond, understanding. Essence is never other than an assumption needed to give the appearance of rationality to what otherwise would remain unintelligible, given existing knowledge at any time. For the purpose in view, it consists in the supposition of some telos in terms of which a development can be represented as having taken place, as systematic and necessary, on the analogy of the finite teleology of production which actually is what such a conception merely purports, and can do no other than merely purport, to be. Since, however, no presumed understanding of the past is possible without this, i.e., no understanding of the present that sets the terms in which historical construction is carried out, the essentialist fallacy is unavoidable. The most that can be done, if historical explanation be sought, is to make an assumption that does not pre-empt the future in any way or the manner of its coming about, viz., that enables the past to be constructed so that the present brings it to its close, without prejudice to any possible radically different future *sui generis* unknowable. The idea of second Nature and homo faber, as the essence and necessary result of the productive form of the human struggle for self-preservation (to restrict matters to this here), attempts this. It tries to explain how these have come to be what they are, how what they are is what they must be, viz., why and in what way they represent the end of a development, however it may be that, for reasons external to them, they may nonetheless continue in being in present fashion, failing the spontaneous generation of a radically new (social) world needed to transform them, one that cannot, in theory or practice, be derived from this essence without self-contradiction.

From this vantage point, the supposition that categorial language is in any way innate in, essential to, "man," becomes untenable, "man" as other than homo faber as we alone can know and experience him, viz., as he has actually been produced by present society, being an expression without any possible content. The supposition, moreover, cannot account for the circumstance that just this mode of language shows signs of breaking down. If, however, it be assumed that categorial language, language grammatically and syntactically structured, owes its creation and production to its being a basic tool of production, of the human struggle for self-preservation, this becomes intelligible. The assumption of second Nature and homo faber permits a development to be charted in terms of the result, the genesis of which it explains, as one leading (relative to what is here in question) to categorial generality, or simplicity, that alters the nature of understanding and *a fortiori*, the linguistic means of its expression, its communication. If Hollywood "history" is to be avoided, it must then be assumed also that this is accompanied by an organic production of the requisite capacities, and doubtless the loss *pari passu* of others. To say then that these capacities are in some manner innate, is but to acknowledge that, being as we are in the world as it is, it is impossible for us to conceive of what man or the world would be like, were these capacities not existent, that the past so constructed as to fall within historical experience makes sense to us only on the supposition of their existence (however undeveloped relative to what has come about), a circumstance easily transformed into a dogmatic assumption about "man". But dogma is not evidence for, let alone proof of, anything. What at most can perhaps be undogmatically held relates to man considered in our own image, as essentially a producer, as homo faber, of other than whom no knowledge and experience is possible, since the world which can be known and experienced is so only in having been produced by homo faber in this form and with this content, which reciprocally has produced him as capable of knowing and experiencing, i.e., of knowing and experiencing it and himself only as so constituted, and of expressing, communicating, this in the only fashion possible, one that is itself a function of that production. The capacity manifested by such language does not escape the fate of other productive capacities. In its categorial mode, language is the vehicle of reason objectified and abstracted, alienated and reified, at whatever stage this may be. It, too, becomes progressively "purer," until, with the advent of modern technology (indeed, in some respects, foreshadowing it), it sheds altogether the form that impedes its complete rationality, language in common use, and, as a tool of production, turns into a mode of communication beyond the unspecialised capacities of homo faber to understand, one in which concepts alone, shorn of gesture, tone, feeling, spontaneous associations, in sum, of everything not appertaining to "purely" rational production, have a place. At this point the correctness mentioned by Vygotsky comes to be definitively achieved as a productive necessity. Luria's investigations into different types of categorial generality, and the capacity for grasping these, in particular the inability to perceive the nature and function of logical classification, strongly support the view of these as, at bottom, deriving from production requirements, and the circumstances directly and indirectly associated with them.

Social production constitutes the world at any stage as rational (something that as said always illicitly encompasses the nonrational that is its particular complement as the world that it is), a rationality expressed and communicated by, *inter alia*, language in its function of means of production. Categorial language is pre-eminently the repository of the rules guiding the activity of productive society, which it expresses in the very structure that makes it the most generally effective vehicle of their communication. To use a language is to affirm the exclusive rules of its world, unconsciously to apprehend, to perceive the world, and thereby oneself, as rational (in the terms rationality happens to have), as second Nature.

31

Of its very nature jussive, the structure of language, like that of all tools, sets the conditions for its employment that have to be learned, submitted to, which submission is one of the basic conditions for membership of society.

So long as homo faber is a necessary agent of production as integral efficient cause and vehicle of the formal cause, production remains at least in principle intelligible to him, the manifestation of his capacities in the form of the objective recollection of its rules repeatedly communicated to him in all his productive and associated activities and their results. Production is (as earlier said) impossible without memory, a capacity that, once created, it develops. So far as the world is rationally apprehensible, it is so as the embodied memory of its productive constitution, the ever-present witness to, and affirmation of, the validity of its rules. To perceive is, in this context, always to remember, unconscious as this remembrance may be, a circumstance that gives point to the Socratic doctrine of knowledge as recollection (however differently expressed). The division and specialisation of labour, of capacities, that forwards production, potentially fractures the integrity of the apprehended, perceived rationality of the world (including that of homo faber). It does not actually do so, however, so long as the world can still be apprehended as the manifestation of the totality of productive capacities that, notwithstanding their specialisation, remain those of homo faber, an integrity categorial language in common use affirms as the general means of their rule-guided communication. So far as the present is concerned (which alone is of interest here), what was potential becomes in principle actual with the emergence of industry, and does so in its consummation in modern technology, production in terms of capacities beyond those of homo faber, that make his increasingly obsolete. The incapacity of homo faber with respect to production that makes its rationality generally unintelligible to him, gradually deprives him of the reflective and reflexive means of becoming himself rational. That the world as perceived becomes non-rational, insofar as both its causality in general cannot be grasped and as the causality of technology becomes unintelligible to the majority of those engaged still in production (and *a fortiori* to those rendered wholly obsolete thereby), entails that homo faber become so. So far as categorial language remains essential to production in the purely rational form appropriate to this, it becomes the preserve of specialists to whom alone it is understandable within the confines of their specialisation. But beyond this it loses its *raison d'être*. In a world that appears the effect of arbitrariness, categorial language, the expression and communication of the rational or rule-guided integrity of the world, loses its function, for all that it remains still in appearance a vehicle of communication. The structure of language in common use, so far as it relates to the basic activity of society, production (self-preservation) in all its ramifications, gradually solidifies into the imperative mood which becomes its own reason simply as fiat, whatever its content, however capricious, at any moment. The loss of productive function that makes homo faber in considerable measure superfluous in the form hitherto required, here manifests itself as the loss of the capacity for reason and for memory associated with it (in sum, of the capacity for learning), other than (where at all) in narrow specialised fields, beyond which irrationality becomes ever more general. Reason, memory, learning as capacities once of homo faber, become also capacities of technology, and transferred to it can be, potentially or actually, developed wholly beyond the limits of homo faber. Contemporary so-called "theories" of education reflect this, in refusing virtually any role in training to what is considered "mechanical". It would be interesting and useful to examine more narrowly the reasons for the failure of educational practice (if educational it may still with propriety be called) based on the idea of the primacy of pleasure and interest as stimuli from the very beginning, at nursery school. But to do so here would involve too lengthy a digression.

III

Before proceeding, some misunderstandings need to be cleared away. One concerns so-called "production for use," taken to be radically different from production for exchange. The distinction is wholly without warrant. It is the outcome of the lack of a concept of second Nature. Properly considered, production for exchange introduces no essential feature not already present in production for use, viz., in production as such. What it does is to bring these to a fuller development, one that in principle would, were it to proceed to its conclusion, wholly eliminate homo faber from production, other than as its indirect controlling and determining agent.

With the, so-to-say "actual" historical development of production I am not concerned. The reconstruction of this process must always be of doubtful validity, owing less to the multitude of accidental circumstances inescapably involved, many of which can later never be known, than to the fact that without some principle of explanation, the choice of which, its determination as that principle, is necessarily in some respects arbitrary, no intelligible development could be at all proposed. In that this principle itself establishes the pattern thereupon imposed, it introduces a hierarchy of causes, some of which are deemed more fundamental than others, a hierarchy for which "history" can give no warrant, since it itself is constituted thereby, the classic modern example being the notoriously unsatisfactory division into sub- and super-structure in however refined a form. In terms of the supposition that every society constitutes an exhaustive hypothesis about itself and its environment, the ascription of essential priority to any of its activities becomes suspect, owing to the (as earlier shown) inescapably anachronistic nature of this procedure. The assertion of the primacy of production, reasonable as this may seem given the primacy of the struggle for self-preservation, already implies a distinction between what is taken to fall into that category and what not, that itself already produces the matter supposedly to be impartially investigated in the desired form with respect to its basic organisation. The very fact that, in being the exhaustive hypothesis it is, and must be, if it is to have a relatively durable stability, a society necessarily constitutes a system, means that in it all particular activities (factors, conditions, however these may be called) conspire to produce the result, that the primacy of some over others is not absolute and permanent, but relative and temporary, the effect of specific, changing circumstances that at one time give an over-riding importance to some, and at another, to others. Taken as a whole for the term of its viable existence, a society produces and reproduces itself through the totality of its activities, none of which can validly be taken as *a priori* more essential than others, so that to ascribe priority to pro-duction is in effect to do no other than to ascribe it to its self-production and reproduction as the society that it is, an assertion of so empty a self-evidence as to be wholly useless.

Aside from, of its very nature, tendentious historical explanation, there remains only the consideration of production itself. The possible objec-tion that this quasi-logical investigation itself pre-supposes a historical development of some kind, the validity of the reconstruction of which has been asserted to be of its nature questionable, is easily shown to lack substance. Such a development, however it be supposed to have taken place, does not itself give production the purposiveness that characterises its mode as an activity, gives it its necessity, i.e., constrains it to be carried on in such a way as answers to the purpose and in no other, if it is to be successful. This, as object of analysis stands in no intrinsic relation to any particular purpose whatever, consequently, is independent of accidental historical circumstances which relate only to the possible sphere of activ-ity, to the (at any time) external limits within which it may be exercised. The production of second Nature and homo faber is a necessity of produc-tion, analysis of which is not furthered, but hampered, so long as it be not freed from irrelevant considerations on the score of alleged historical realism and accuracy. In fine, production is an activity that has intrinsic features that themselves stamp all its results with a character deriving from its very exercise, no matter what adventitious conditions may obtain, or how such conditions may affect the form of appearance of the results.

That production is of its very nature purposive means that it is for use, whatever this use may be, something irrelevant to production as such. Exchange, for instance, is a use no different in this connection from any other. The classification that refuses this title to exchange does not derive from the nature of production properly considered. It derives from some arbitrary assumption about what constitutes use relative to such need as can supposedly be called human, a judgment that itself issues from some equally unwarranted dogmatic notion of human nature as, in some fan-cied respect, an essential constant unrelated to production (or related to it only externally), one that in these alleged fundamental respects deter-mines production which so far is asserted to be "natural". That this view is wholly without foundation will be clear from what was earlier shown to be the necessary character of production in its inseparable connection with the emergence of homo faber, viz., in connection with need and human nature, so far as these can at all be objects of knowledge, as exclusively the needs and nature of homo faber as produced at any time, which themselves constitute the foundation of all judgments concerning them. The commonly received notion of production for use has plainly nothing to do with use as a category of production, but bespeaks the consideration of production (itself taken for granted without further thought) in terms of some or other criterion external to it. That this criterion itself, though with respect to the analysis of production extraneous, is nonetheless determined by production, in the sense that any criterion whatsoever is ultimately derivable only from such suggestions about "human nature" as the actually produced homo faber nature permits, is something about which enough has been said. Here what is pertinent is the exhibition of the inevitable confusion and error resulting from the uncritical importation of such a criterion (or of such criteria) into the analysis of production.

One instance is the radical disjunction taken for granted between production for use and for exchange, in the form of the supposed difference between their modes of procedure, co-operation, and competition respectively. In actuality, however, production as such is necessarily competitive in its fundamental relation to the unknown original, out of which the sphere proper to it, that of second Nature, is (after an initial spontaneously arisen creative intuition) produced and reproduced by appropriation (together with its complement, unknowable first Nature). The very circumstance that production is an expression of the struggle for self-preservation gives competition primacy over co-operation (exceptions granted). Kropotkin's attempt to restore to co-operation its supposed primacy "in normal conditions" is an error. Co-operation can normally never be more than a witting or unwitting element within the inescapable general context of competition that gives production one of its inherent characteristics. Insofar as co-operation is internal to production, it is no more than a technical requirement of its procedure, the requirement that the several activities involved be carried on in a determinate concerted manner relative to the realisation of the purpose in view. All production is inherently co-operative in the sense that the material, the efficient, the formal and the final causes must all work together under the general direction of the last. In relation, however, to a so-called "balance" between society and its environment, and that out of which these have been first created and subsequently produced and reproduced by appropriation, that is, to the achievement of a relative stability between them, co-operation is wholly external to production (exceptions once more granted). Where such a state is (perhaps questionably) said to be perceived (in, for example, what Levi-Strauss calls the "cold" societies) it can be nothing but the outcome of a determined limitation of production to what experience (trial and error) suggests is compatible with such stability, so long as no circumstances beyond social prevision and control arise. It is, that is, the outcome of a judgment about what quantum of disturbance the unknown original out of which society and its environment have been produced by appropriation can bear, without destroying the possibility of continued production of second Nature (including homo faber) in the given form and content. The judgment is necessarily arbitrary, and though the outcome of experiment never has and never can have the force of necessity, since, from the standpoint of knowledge and experience, it is inescapably one-sided, restricted to what has been produced, aside from which all is unknown and some of it unknowable, owing to the very activity of production itself. Here co-operation represents an act of will that stands in no necessary relation to production at all, and indeed in no way alters the fact that production itself remains fundamentally competitive with respect to that with which co-operation is one-sidedly sought for the sake of stability and continuance of second Nature. The supposition that it has a fatality about it deriving from the "co-operative" nature of "production for use" that would *eo ipso* limit production and make the associated needs equally limited, and thereby more satisfiable easily (than is possible in present "complex" competitive society) is a romantic, not to say, nostalgic illusion associated with the condescending view of "primitive" peoples as children, creatures of instinct rather than reason, and on that account "closer" to "Nature". In reality, however, the limited development of production constitutes the given limited second Nature and homo faber nature merely in the sense of the sphere of possible productive activity, possible need. It does not of itself limit the quantum of such activity within this sphere, nor that of the satisfaction of need (the extent to which need is judged licit), activity, and satisfaction which, with equal lack of necessity relative to production itself may just as well involve reckless, as conservative, exploitation. Whatever limitation may at any time and in any such society have been selected, and however this determination may have been achieved in actuality, it represents a conscious act not to be dismissed as what it is, a choice among a set of equally necessary (or unnecessary) possibilities, one the difficulty of reaching we may not, for lack of any possible knowledge and experience of what this involved, make light of, on the presumed score of its being mere "child's play" compared with the unwarrantedly assumed greater present difficulties of so doing.

The supposition the mistaken idea of production for use leads to, that a return to it (which, as a return to something that has never existed as alleged, is already nonsensical), is a *sine qua non* for the establishment of freedom and happiness as the defining character of social life is simply an illusion grounded in the thoughtless belief that competition is extrinsic to production and capable of being wholly done away with, that the struggle for existence is but a temporary phase in "man's" social evolution. Such a view entirely overlooks the distinction between the relations that hold within a society, and its relations as a whole that, as second Nature, it inescapably must have to the original. The most varied internal social relations, the most varied forms of the struggle for self-preservation within a society, are self-evidently compatible with production, without in any way altering the fact that every society as such, as a particular constituted second Nature, has, and can have, no other than a competitive relation to the original that forms the context within which it necessarily produces and reproduces itself in the only manner possible, by the appropriation, the creative and productive transformation of portions of that original into second Nature. This comprehensive social struggle for self-preservation is independent of all purely internal relations. Far from being a mere phase, it is an inescapable fatality, the intrinsic violence and aggression of which (i.e., competition) can possibly be reduced (as apparently in the "cold" societies) but never overcome. Production is with respect to man (to confine myself to him here) the manner in which the struggle for self-preservation has to be carried on. It not merely in general determines the relations he, as homo faber, enters into; it also debars him, *qua* homo faber, from all possibility of having radically different relations, relations not directly or indirectly stemming from the struggle for self-preservation that sets the overriding limits to his nature as producer, however differently this may manifest itself in particular in different societies.

What lies beyond these limits, owes nothing to anything of which we can have experience and knowledge, is self-evidently unknowable to us. It follows that the attempt to come to grips with this, relative to a possible future freedom, within the context of aesthetics (as by Schiller, for instance, and, more recently, Marcuse) is basally in error, suggestive as it may appear. Its ground is the supposition that the sphere of aesthetics does not (as it actually does) appertain to production, that it has actual, not merely fancied, illusory, reference to man as other than homo faber, and gives, within the "kingdom of necessity," some substantial, if qualified, foreknowledge of freedom, something altogether impossible in view of the absolute mutual exclusion of production and freedom that makes knowledge of freedom a self-contradiction, and its description in the only terms available, those of categorial, rule-structured, language, an absurdity, brilliant as the attempt may be (Oscar Wilde's, for example).

A further error deriving from the mistaken idea of "production for use" as a mode of production, one peculiarly geared, supposedly, to the satisfaction of ("true") need, is the belief that it has, in keeping with this alleged circumstance, a humane character compatible with "freedom", absent from production for exchange. Production, however, as earlier shown, has inherent constraints always at work, whatever may be the accidental, historical conditions in which it is carried on, conditions that may, and indeed do, bring about forms of inhumanity peculiar to themselves, not essential to production as such. Were these latter to be wholly absent, this would in no way affect production itself, which would still require the subjection of man *qua* agent in whatever way this might be, to its finite teleological necessity, as an essential condition of its successful achievement. The production, for example, of eunuchs and castrati, of dwarves and grotesques, may be considered a historical accident. But the physical and mental deformations brought about by the division and specialisation of labour arise out of production itself as its unavoidable concomitants, and stamp it as inherently inhumane, a fact that supports the Greek view of labour as unworthy of free men, as incompatible with freedom. In effect, from the standpoint of freedom, there is no difference whatever between so-called production for use and production for exchange. Technology does away with the need for the most crass of these deformations (at least in principle), without in the least altering the fact that in the realm of finite teleology, the telos is king, and any relation to it involves not just subjection, but subjection in the appropriate form, i.e., some quantum of deformation, physical and mental, but for which production would not be possible. That production remains always a necessity imposed by the never-to-be overcome struggle for self-preservation (however this may be kept in bounds by a determination to restrict the sorts of needs to the satisfaction of which production is required, as well as the degree to which these may safely be satisfied), indicates that to some, in prospect indeterminable, extent and manner subjection and the accompanying deformation must ever be an aspect of human existence, insofar as man in some fashion, however indirect, must necessarily be involved in production. This has nothing to do with how satisfying in one fashion or another, owing partly to individual tastes and aptitudes, partly to the conditions in which it is carried on, work may be, a quantum of which will presumably always remain a need, expressive of the fact that homo faber nature must always remain a constituent of man, however subordinate a place it may have in a human nature determined by the requirements of life beyond production. Given the appropriate circumstances, the achievement of a purpose can make the subjection to the necessity thereto required a thoroughly rewarding experience. But the most satisfying subjection remains subjection nonetheless, a fact that elucidates Marx's error in supposing that freedom in its proper acceptation arises from, or is associated with, *inter alia*, the mere absence of constraint upon choice of occupation, once this is no longer connected with livelihood; for, more pleasing as it undoubtedly may be to be able to fish, hunt, etc., from choice, when one wills, it remains that fishing, hunting, etc., are disciplines necessarily carried on "under the guidance of rules" (and the more expertly, the more strictly), forms of production which, in the most ideal conditions imaginable, can have no possible relation to freedom so understood at all. It does, of course, have a relation to freedom defined in conventional terms as a condition characterised by a certain amplitude of, to all appearances, unconstrained choice, as, as one might say, a relaxed mode of servitude.

The final error to be dealt with here is the outcome of the others: the supposition that production for use in its connection with alleged "essential" human needs finds its automatic limit in the "natural" limit to consumption, such that, without conscious intervention, the time to be apportioned to production is necessarily, or "naturally", abridged. Underlying this is an assumption that notwithstanding all social factors, there is at bottom some unalterable biological specification of need that will in these circumstances assert itself as the determining factor. If the view has any substance at all, it is in the sense of being the presumption of an utter crudity of need, need as such (which is all that can be asserted of biological need, with respect to man at least, to go no further here), an abstraction unknown, except perhaps in artificial conditions of imposed extreme want (concentration camps, labour camps).

What is "natural" with reference to need is, however, never other than what appertains to "man" in terms of the human nature any society gives rise to as part of its total self-preservative, self-reproductive activities. Such a human nature, which is a feature of the general hypothesis any society constitutes, namely, of the world as exclusively perceivable, knowable, and experiencible to it, is itself a determining condition of production, as much as it is reciprocally determined by it, a circular process expressive of the irrefragable limits of all possibilities set by the constitutive social hypothesis itself. Need is not determined by production as such, for all that produced second Nature sets the bounds both of possible need and of the possibility of its satisfaction at any time in conjunction with its accordant homo faber nature; nor does production as such, other perhaps than exceptionally in conditions that bespeak a temporary or permanent break-up of a second Nature, contain anything that could itself limit need in kind or amount within these bounds. The multiplicity of accidental circumstances that conspires to give any society its actual features (including its specific production), to make it a particular, selective expression of the general, abstract possibilities to which second Nature and accordant homo faber nature give rise, have a similar effect on needs, as these actually manifest themselves. There is almost no end to the variety of needs history records (which, given its peculiar nature, may be categorically said not to comprise the sum of needs that have existed), many of which it is almost impossible to associate in any way with any concept of production (in its narrow, conventional tendentious acceptation) as their determining factor, however remote and ultimate this may be said to be. Within a given social context, no distinction arises among needs that would allow some to be properly deemed essential or "true" and other inessential or "false." The difficulty in persuading people to eat what they are not accustomed to (wheat, for instance, instead of rice) shows that even needs that might be supposed to be *a priori* essential in "biological" terms and *in abstracto* indiscriminately satisfiable, are (at least within limits) essential in actuality only in their accepted and acceptable form which, if denied, can turn them into inessential ones; just as, contrariwise,

40

needs that by the same token might be considered inessential (so-called "spiritual" ones) can turn out to be so essential, that their denial can result in the loss of the will to live. Where such distinctions are made, they bespeak either a criticism resulting from some relatively profound change in society affecting attitudes to what was formerly taken for granted, or a judgment passed by a different society in the light of the different homo faber nature that there prevails, the ground of which is plainly extrinsic to the needs in question. Needs that are taken for granted as "in the nature of things" in whatever sense this may be at any time, constitute their own self-evident standard of fitness. That a moral aspect comes at all to be associated with need as something discussable, shows it to have become in some respect questionable.

From the standpoint of crude biological need associated with self-preservation as such (an abstraction merely), all actual need as socially determined upon criteria that *sui generis* go beyond this constitute an excess, as does the consumption satisfying it. Indeed production itself, as an interference with the unknown original always accompanied by un-knowable residues (first Nature), is, relative to this original, likewise an excess, as it is in its very mode of standardisation of procedure, material, and capacity that gives it the possibility of extension and variation in response to social factors wholly unconnected with any abstract biologi-cal need. In fine society, the sum of relations necessarily established by the manner in which the human struggle for self-preservation has to take place, is eo ipso the theatre (so to say) of excess. The circumstance, an ineluctable condition, is in itself of no practical significance in normal cir-cumstances in any society, and never shows itself in this general fashion at all. How excess manifests itself *in concreto*, and what its effects are, especially relative to ideas about radical social change, are matters to be considered. Here, all that is pertinent is its elucidation in abstraction from all particularity owed to historical circumstances, as a corrective to the erroneous view that "production for use" and supposedly associated need and consumption are, in contradistinction to production for exchange and its associated needs, intrinsically preservative of the proper measure established "by nature."

Exchange as use has one feature that distinguishes it from all other particular uses. It constitutes use in general, wholly abstracted from all specific form and thus in principle capable of unlimited extension such that it itself becomes the single purpose of production as a whole, partic-ular uses functioning merely as so many of its manifestations. This gener-ality gives production for exchange its unifying factor, makes it systematic in a manner wholly impossible before. In the strict sense of the term "system", that of a totality organised on the basis of a single principle, present society appears to constitute the nearest approach to being (in the narrow conventional sense) a productive system that has ever existed, one that is, apparently, determined at bottom by purely economic criteria.

It is this peculiarity, the fact that (so far as so narrowly conceived a system can actually ever be said to exist) production in this narrow sense appears really to be its fundamentally determining factor, that has made possible the reconstruction of history in the anachronistic terms of economic determinism. This, illuminating as it is in certain respects (so far, that is, as semblance can be so), not only raises insoluble problems, but, more to the point, in its nature of historical explanation bound to encompass all accidentality as possible causal factors, can never come to rest in a definitive statement the necessity of which is rationally defensible, i.e., capable of being established without resort to ultimate self-evidence, the hallmark of dogma that philosophy of history vainly labours to justify as reasonable.

All historical representation (as said) results from the imposition of some imputed necessity upon material which, but for that, must be for us thoroughly fortuitous, a necessity in terms of which its causality can be produced and given an appearance of intelligibility that permits of its being bodied forth as a development. Whether there be anything in this material itself that might, even though only analogically, be deemed necessity, it is impossible to surmise, since the only form and content in which we can become aware of it at all, i.e., even as no more than having the capacity for being the needed material, involves the imputation of some principle of explanation, but for which it must remain wholly senseless to us. History never happens. It is always produced. Indeed, it is precisely history, the form in which we necessarily must represent the past to ourselves as rationally apprehensible (even if this is no more than an appearance), that makes it impossible to determine what actually happened, i.e., to discover what relation (if any) the representation we produce as history has to this, that in the very terms of historical production becomes a priori unknowable to us. Historical development is of its nature illusion, albeit perhaps one required by reason itself, so long at least as society as a whole remain unmastered, and suffering demand justification. The illusion of rationality can be seen in Marx's hypothetical account of the emergence of the "propertyless worker" associated with the definitive establishment of production for exchange, the moment it be asked what there is in property and production that permitted either of these results to come about at all, i.e., the moment the nature of what Marx makes his starting point (something which, to avoid the infinite regress that would make explanation impossible, he must take to be self-evident fact), comes to be inquired into.

The unsatisfactoriness of this starting point lies not in any question of historical fact, as if some other more appropriate could be suggested. It lies in the very circumstance of its being both historical and factual, something that would be so of any alternative of the same kind proposed. In the context of explanation (alone pertinent here) facts are constructs, always contingent upon some hypothesis which allows of their production, and limited to what it makes perceptible and knowable, thus always of debatable validity. Every new hypothesis necessarily both produces new facts and destroys old ones (denies them the status of fact), constructing a reality and actuality in accord with itself as informing principle. To remove the unsatisfactoriness of Marx's starting point requires then that there be adduced something that owes nothing to historical representation, that cannot be considered as arising within the terms of any development, can never be given the status of fact, something that occurs independently of all possible accidental circumstances (however, these may affect its form of manifestation), i.e., occurs in the very nature of man's self-preservative activity and itself is involved in the production of history and its facts, as one of its determining conditions. The analysis of production so far as it has here gone suggests that something of this kind can be elucidated from it.

Abstraction and objectification (reification and alienation), the manner in which the capacities of what come to be second Nature and homo faber nature are first created and then produced and reproduced involve the constitution of these as property in the double sense of character and belonging. The creation and subsequent production of "food", for instance, represents its constitution not only as that which has this objectified property (manifests this capacity objectively), but also as that which has been wrested (abstracted) from the unknown original, and henceforth, in this reified and alienated form, as "food", and as such only, belongs to man as his property; just as do the cognitive and perceptive activities therewith bound up which likewise, and in like fashion, as abtracted and objectified (i.e., reified and alienated), and so alone, become produced properties (capacities), and the property of man. Property is an integral feature of production as such, a necessary form of man's relation to what he constitutes as nature for himself and in himself, by reason of the way in which his activity of self-preservation has to be carried on, a form that exhibits the whole, as produced, to be through and through social. The essential social character of second Nature and homo faber nature does not derive from any accidental historical circumstance, for all that this gives it varying expression, but manifests the fact that neither is originally given, that both are exclusively a result of the activity of abstraction and objectification which creates and (re-)produces them in the only form possible, as reified and alienated property (properties). Even were the activity resulting in the constitution of "food" in the form of property and accordant properties to be supposed that of an isolated individual, this would, *pace* Marx's objection to Robinson Crusoe, nowise alter its social nature which resides wholly in the fact of its having been, of its having had to be, produced, if it was to be at all. The relations established by production are social not because men constitute one of their terms, but because it can (in its very nature) give rise to no relations at all other than in terms of some constituted property (or properties) of man and material. That is to say, independently of all historical accident, social relations are of their nature property relations.

The ascription of the emergence of property to historical causes is the source of endless irremediable confusion, among which the supposed distinction between private and other forms of ownership (however called). In reality, the fundamental relation constituted by second Nature, that in terms of which alone it comes about simultaneously with first Nature, viz., appropriation or abstraction, stamps property as intrinsically private. But for this circumstance, ownership in no matter what fashion could never have come about, would be inconceivable. It is the fact that second Nature and homo faber nature are necessarily produced in the form of abstraction and objectification, in other words, in such reified and alienated form as inherently lends itself to being appropriated (it itself being as merely the possibility of what it has become, already the result of an original appropriation), that permits of their being owned. Property is private not because it is (inequitably) owned by individual persons; it is owned (whatever the manner) because it is *in se* private. There is no basal difference between so-called public and private ownership with respect to the private character of property which is unalterable, residing in its very nature of property, something not affected by any external, adventitious circumstance determining the particular manner of ownership.

Property relations are both necessary and accidental. As the former, they comprise those every society, however specific its mode of the production of second Nature and homo faber nature may be, sustains one-sidedly to the unknown original out of which it has been constituted by abstraction (appropriation). In this respect, society is *sui generis* the sphere of property, of ownership of that in terms of which it makes itself what it is, an ownership that is private with respect to society as a whole in the relation(s) mentioned. Which is to say, society is impossible other than as the private appropriation of that which, if not so abstracted and objectified, so created and re-produced, would (and could) not exist at all. The difference between mine and yours (one of the grounds of identity) inheres in society at its very beginning as, in the first instance, the distinction between second Nature and the unknown original, inseparable from the act of creation and production as such that gives rise to it.

Within this general framework, the property relations internal to any society are the result of accidental circumstances that determine who owns what and how that ownership is expressed. These may change; indeed have done so; but no change of any kind in these can affect the fundamental property character of society as such, which remains what it is independently of all the vicissitudes of history.

The reification and alienation intrinsic to property manifest themselves clearly in the fact that property shares the paradoxical character of inversion observable in production. Just as the latter involves the subjection of the producer to its rules, so *mutatis mutandis* does property, the owner. The distinction and opposition between individual and society noted by

Marx arises out of the very nature of property (of production), which, as fundamental social relation, itself first possesses him who would possess any part of it. To belong to society (however at anytime defined, and whatever the form the belonging may take) is the condition of having any part of the property (and properties) it gives rise to in the course of its self-preservative activities. Society, the sphere of property, is inherently that of subjection to rule that determines (limits) behaviour. The classicism of production earlier noted, the manifestation of its intrinsic generality or rationality, attaches to all its effects, self-evidently then to the society that is the organised expression of the totality of activities directly and indirectly connected with production (self-preservation). What behaviour is proper to any society, what accords with its property (or production) requirements, conforms to rule, that is, and in this is for it alone rational, is thus inescapably standard, conventional. Spontaneity, radically excluded from production owing to its very mode of procedure, is likewise excluded from society, other than as an aberration, albeit in important respects a necessary and unavoidable one.

To define man in classical fashion as a social animal, as become himself only as object for, and subject to, rule (then alone neither brute nor god) is to fall into the error of inductive generalisation without title to necessity. The fact that no knowledge or experience of man (as homo faber) is at all possible other than in terms of rule, that any rational apprehension and comprehension of him has of necessity to take this form, transforms such a definition into a *petitio principi* expressive of the absolute limits of all such knowledge and experience, without prejudice to what (if anything) man may otherwise be. In effect, all possible knowledge and experience of man is unalterably restricted to what he has produced himself to be, to man as homo faber, in which form his condition is necessarily servile, and just in this manifests itself as social. Society, properly considered, is the form of organisation peculiar not to man as such, but to man as homo faber, subordinated in all essential respects to the imperative requirements of self-preservation, unfree as producer of property, sc. of himself as property, whether as owner or non-owner; as it is, in connection with its environment, peculiar to second Nature in its capacity of mere material for that production, that self-preservation.

Aristotle's definition is correct in asserting that such servitude is a fatality, so far as man is involved in production, so far as his existence is social, determined by the requirements of self-preservation; and underscores the fact that, if man is to be free (in the strict acceptation of this term), it can only be beyond the confines of self-preservation. Logically, thus, the possibility may be deduced of a mode of life beyond property, beyond ownership, in sum, beyond society, (or, what is the same, beyond production in the comprehensive signification given it here). But what this might be we have no means at all of discovering, wholly limited as we are, by the very nature of our knowledge and experience, to that which

45

can be brought within the compass of rule, not indeed rule in general (the *sine qua non* of knowledge and experience as such), but that specific to our society as exhaustive second Nature and homo faber nature hypothesis, the nature of which, its limits, can itself (as earlier argued) be neither known nor experienced. This purely logical possibility of a non-social mode of life, one that, being altogether beyond rule, would be free, with its implications for human nature other than that of homo faber, is, and can be, of no practical utility to us, having reference to a wholly unknowable future radically different from the present. Yet, for all that it can be, for us, in connection with any such possible future, no more than a bare abstraction the validity of which can in no conceivable fashion be put to the test, there being no possible conditions that could allow of its being done, it nevertheless, as a logical supposition, provides a standpoint from which ideas about human nature currently accepted can be critically examined, shown to be necessarily erroneous in their unquestioned generality for lack of a concept of second Nature and homo faber nature, albeit that here again their intrinsic one-sidedness can be merely asserted *in abstracto*, there being no means at all of establishing what it consists in *in concreto*, and possibility of correcting it.

With this, the examination of production as such, so far as here relevant, is complete. No more was required than to show that production *sui generis* has necessary characteristics that stamp all its effects, independently of all accidental historical circumstances which do no more than determine the manner in which they manifest themselves.

IV

If we now consider modern society, it is plain that it exhibits these characteristics, abstraction and objectification (reification and alienation), the constitution of all properties to which it gives rise, whether of man or material, as property, competition, servitude (in the form of general "wage slavery" coupled with universal exchange), inversion (Marx's "commodity fetishism"), excess, to a marked extent. This results from the fact that, owing to a peculiar concatenation of accidental circumstances, production has been developed to the point at which, seemingly, second Nature actually constitutes a potentially systematic whole (as against its more or less obvious mere semblance of rationality heretofore), one that, in appearance, has, to all intents and purposes, supplanted "Nature" in its common acceptation of mere raw material. This development is reflected in the shift from the critical stance of Kant to the, in this respect, virtually, realist one shared by Hegel and Marx, notwithstanding their opposed starting points. It is, however, just in this that, upon critical examination, second Nature shows itself with respect to this supposition to be rational semblance, the very completeness of which prevents its being perceived as such, so long as production be taken not as constitutive, but eductive merely, of "Nature".

The acceptance of second Nature at face value, as if it were Nature simply, is one of the sources of the absolute sterility of social theory (especially of the so-called "progressive"), caught in a vicious circle of which it is not even aware. It can be seen to advantage in Marx.

One of the cardinal errors of *Capital* as social theory (it being as strictly economic theory of no particular interest here) is the assumption that the method used is scientific (in which it reproduces the mistaken idea of science arising from the untenable reflection theory of consciousness), that the work consists in the elucidation of the laws of motion of society, taken to be actual existents (clouded as they may be from common view), by means of appropriate empirical investigation. There is, however, no way at all in which such a representation can be accepted as this, if the

47

term "law" is to retain anything of its proper signification. Whatever the sphere of its operation, "law" is the expression of control, of the establishment of conditions amenable to, thus themselves the product of, rule, that which alone makes them (and it) rational. It falls wholly within the compass of finite teleology, of that which has been produced in such fashion as can be summarily expressed in the form of a law (or of laws) governing the processes involved. To say that anything is governed by law is but another way of saying that we know it to have come about under the guidance of rule, because we ourselves have produced, as an instance, an effect, of the pertinent rule, what was initially, of course, but an untested hypothesis advanced as a possibly rational means to that end; just as, conversely, the fact that it has been so produced is the *sine qua non* of our knowing it, of its having the rational form proper to comprehension, viz., as that of which, other than so produced (whatever this may be), we can have no possible knowledge at all. Knowledge is of its nature lawful or rational only because it is, and can never be other than, something, the lawfulness or rationality of which has actually been established, that is to say, given independent existence as objective and objectified, a result that comes about only as the conclusion of trial and error.

The phrase "law of motion" is strictly a pleonasm, law as *summa summarum* of a process of production being the general form of expression of the relations established (or where the process of production is uncertain, tentatively put forward as holding) among the factors of production brought together for the purpose, viz., of the several motions these have been definitively or experimentally determined to perform with respect to one another to that end. Motion is never other than determinate, specific, a character that stamps it only in virtue of its having been so produced in conformity with some purpose to the achievement of which it is to be used. Even as wholly hypothetical motion (which every one necessarily is to begin with), it is a specific suggestion whereby we try to represent to ourselves the production of something, the *modus operandi* of which is not known, in such fashion as we initially surmise this to be capable of being brought about. A motion imparted to what is assumed to be the relevant factors is an aspect of the purpose proposed, translated into that concatenation of acts conceived as leading of its realisation, whether that conception or that concatenation be correct being established strictly and only by trial and error.

The so-called "laws of motion" exhibited in *Capital* are not of this kind at all, their elucidation having precisely the opposite intention, of showing that they are that in virtue of which society is of its very nature out of control. The contradiction is plain: Motion being nothing but a means of control, and only coming to be, and to be known, as so produced, there can be no motion of any kind that could be determined as objective, objectified, as knowable, and as such attributable to what is *sui generis* beyond control. The very fact that that which is beyond control is so, signifies that no knowledge of it is either presently available or at all possible, that whatever it may be either does not for the time being, or never can, fall within the compass of finite teleology with which alone motion is associated as an object of knowledge. In short, of that to which motion cannot be attributed (in the sense described), no determinate processes can be predicated, such as would permit it to be represented in intelligible terms (other than as semblance, the illusory nature of which manifests itself so soon as practical measures of control are called for). Whatever it may be, it asserts itself as a fatality, submission to which is unavoidable, so that what description we may give of it once clear of semblance (since describe it we must, if only as unintelligible) has reference only to our wholly one-sided relation to it, not to any possible relation it may have to us (or whether it have any relation at all), to know which would be to determine it in some fashion as having at least those properties premised by such a relation or possibility of relation, a determination that would bring it, to that extent, out of the realm of fatality into that of (at least possible) control. In sum, that whatever it may be asserts itself as a fatality means that it either is not or cannot ever be an object for knowledge, a circumstance to which Schopenhauer gave striking expression in the remark that death cannot be experienced (anymore, it must be added, than can creation), something that holds as much for societies as for individual persons or organisms.

The self-contradiction intrinsic to *Capital* as social history is due only in part to the erroneous concept of scientific method that informs the work, one that, however, has itself a curious result. The method that Marx derives from Hegel purports to describe the movement of that which is investigated, as if it were inherent in it independently of such investigation that, if correct, reduces itself to description. That is to say, whatever activity be involved in arriving at this correct picture, the stance that betokens successful achievement is one of passive contemplation of that which has been elucidated as the inner necessity that determines the development and brings it to its appointed end, one that, owing to its attributed essential inherence, can nowise be altered anymore than can in any basal respect the development it prescribes, do what men will. In terms, then, of its method, which patently cannot be squared with the demand of the Feuerbach thesis, its intrinsic (reflective) stance being wholly incompatible with the requirements of (revolutionary) praxis, *Capital*, if correct, should be the proof of the impossibility of conscious radical social change, the *decursus vitae* of society being in essence unalterable, and its features, whatever men may do, but phenomenal forms through which the inner necessity fatally establishes itself. In Marx, as in Hegel, the reflection theory as methodological principle concludes in the assertion of the powerlessness of men against fate. But fate once admitted, its manner of coming-to-be ceases to be of interest with respect to it, since, be it thus or otherwise, nothing different can ultimately result.

49

It is of interest only to the extent that some or other temporary accommodation be sought within these irrefrangible limits. (In like manner, the manner of death is irrelevant with respect to the fact that death cannot be avoided; it is of interest only with respect to the quantum of suffering that may be experienced by the dying.) Relative to society, as to Nature, the reflection theory of consciousness leads to the conclusion that reform alone is within the capacity of man. Yet *Capital* arises out of the criticism of philosophy as merely descriptive and functions in Marx's view as a tool, as an indispensable element of (revolutionary) praxis.

This incompatibility, real given the reflection theory as premise, whence the insuperable difficulties Marxist theory has in allowing for and accounting for spontaneity, reveals itself to be but an appearance, if this theory be set aside, if, that is, *Capital* be seen to be not a reflection of some independently existing actuality, but the production of a seeming actuality falsely taken to have independent existence. In its very nature of analysis, *Capital* is determined by the purpose (or pre-supposed synthesis) directing the procedure to a representation accordant with itself, one which constitutes reality and its facts as fit for the purpose. That purpose for Marx is revolution and the guidance of activity thereto. Many of the basal categories of this representation are found already in the *Communist Manifesto*, and some even in the earlier *1844 Manuscripts*, as are (implicitly) the logical categories assumed to depict correctly the essential process of development in Nature and society as one leading necessarily to qualitative (in social terms, revolutionary) change. However many difficulties Marx may have grappled with as economist, owing to the refusal of circumstances to accord with what social theory demanded, and however many qualifications this led him to introduce inconsistent with it, as a social thinker he kept to the representation of capitalist society as one teleologically determined by revolution as its terminus, a fact productive of confusion and contradiction, however one looks at *Capital*, whether as economic or social theory or (most unrewardingly) as both without distinction. Thus, whereas Adorno's remark that from *Capital* it is impossible to learn how to make a revolution is correct relative to it as economic theory, it is wholly incorrect relative to it as social theory, and taken to refer to it altogether prevents a critical consideration of the work from this aspect.

The process of development Marx accepts is Hegel's (granted their opposing starting points), the progression from potentiality to actuality, whereby that which was implicitly necessary manifests itself explicitly as such in the course of becoming what it shows itself thereby to have been destined to be. It is through the complete *decursus vitae*, which alone fully constitutes that which has developed as what it is, that the potentiality becomes capable of being cognised as the telos determining the entire development, which from this retrospective vantage point exhibits itself as a system. For Marx, as for Hegel, only when so systematic can knowledge of anything be said to be scientific.

The model for this representation is production, the supposed intrinsic movement of which it purports to set forth *in abstracto*. It is in intention the exhibition of what might be called the logic of the process of production in exemplary form, without reference to any particular end. Just this is what today deprives the result of all title to science, to knowledge. A production process is specific to that which it is intended to produce. A description of it as a mode of procedure is no other than the series of instructions about what to do with the pertinent material and agents in order to achieve the desired end, which end not merely determines the procedure but also what is to constitute the material and agent, what their nature must be relative to it. Even where such instructions take the form of law (or, where production involves several distinct processes, materials and agents, laws), such procedural generalisation remains of limited applicability, having reference only to that production of which it is the summary expression, and governing only that, viz., only to the operations and material (or materials) and agent (or agents) in question. These instructions constitute its logic, to express which in more abstract terms, i.e., as an instance of causality, would clearly be pointless in this specific connection, whatever might conceivably be its usefulness in others. This is so relative to production as such which, as other than an activity the nature and results of which can properly be examined in themselves, is but a name for the sum of production processes, not one itself. The supposition that it is, that it constitutes, as it were, the pattern of process itself, analysis of which would reveal the essential movement involved, to which all particular known processes can be seen at least broadly to conform as instances, is, however, originally no aberration. It is the outcome of reflection grounded in the belief that the world is so constituted as to be rationally apprehensible, i.e., as rational in itself, despite the apparent sheer fortuity of its ceaseless coming-to-be and withering away. It is fundamental to the attempt (the first comprehensive statement of which is found in Aristotle's doctrine of the four causes) to make intelligible what has not been (or cannot be) produced, on the assumption that it has been, even if not by men, and that its production must exhibit the features obtaining in all actual production processes, features which here have perforce to be expressed in accordant general or formal terms (as abstract categories) to which no determinate content can be attributed. This is, as said before, the illicit extension of reason, rational semblance, now first in terms seemingly proper to reason itself that mask its illusory nature.

Hegel's reformulation of this first representation of process in general (dialectics) discards the idea of origin as itself unmoved, that prevents its being fashioned into a system. The difficulty associated with the idea of origin in terms of Being and Nothing vanishes, so soon as this is seen as at once the premise and consequence of a systematic representation which would not be so, were it not all-inclusive, circular, from which it

51

follows that with respect to system as conceived thus, it becomes quite immaterial whether it be considered as in motion or at rest, there being no external point of vantage relative to which its condition as the one or the other becomes determinable. The supposition that it be in the one or other condition depends then on the purpose to be served, that decides which of the two is appropriate in the circumstances, without prejudice to the appropriateness of the other in other circumstances. The effect is absolutely to bar all possibility of change (development) to system itself, in consequence of which its logical priority as potentiality—entailing the ascription of ontological existence to Mind (or in the materialist version that bespeaks but a formal alteration in what is taken to be the locus of origin, to Matter)—must be assumed, an assumption that, for its part, limits all possibility of alteration just as absolutely to that therein implicitly contained *ab origine*. It is only within such limits inhering in the very nature of system so defined that change (motion, development) can be determined as occurring, the result of which overall can *ex hypothesi* be nothing other than the actualising of that of which system was initially but the potentiality. That is, system was at first both in appearance Nothing and at the same time in principle everything, viz., it had some, as yet empty, Being. System being exclusive, its development into what it potentially is which, in the nature of the case, can only be internal, can take place only as a movement between its initial states which begins the process of its self-development that gradually explicates the content at first hidden, but in Being.

System itself, other than as all-inclusive, is not capable of representation, not being something separable from its self-development. Its only possible representation is in terms of that development, to which alone the categories, the conceptual form necessarily taken by a description of process in general, refer. To assert that this same development can (or worse, must) simultaneously result in a qualitative (or radical) change whereby system itself is transformed into something quite other, is thus to lapse into illogic, the very idea of systematic development here in question having as its premise the unchangeability of system itself as wholly determining (limiting) potentiality, but for which there would be no terms in which it could at all be rationally conceived (albeit but as semblance), elucidated as necessary.

The error of objective idealism and dialectical materialism stemming from their respective ontological pre-suppositions is to make development in general exemplary in the form of infinite teleology, of which the finite teleology that characterises human production is but a copy, whether men are aware of this or not. The reverse, however, is all that experience allows to be asserted. No perception, no knowledge, is possible other than that arising, directly or indirectly, out of production. Finite teleology is not merely the necessary form productive activity takes; it is also that in which perception, experience, and knowledge come to be.

Perception and knowledge, and experience, are thus of their very nature hypothetical, owing to the manner in which they alone arise, and can arise, however appearance may suggest otherwise. They are what they are (and can alone be) only through the medium of a hypothesis that, as the expression of some purpose, produces that which becomes perceivable, knowable, and capable of being experienced, in the objective and objectified form thereto requisite, a form that bespeaks no relation to anything supposedly existing independently of that hypothesis, but is such only in terms of it, as one of its effects. Only what is and can be so produced as objective and objectified ranks as fact, is part of the reality, and actuality, the hypothesis constitutes.

So far as concerns the general, fundamental social hypotheses specifically here in question (of which those Kuhn calls "paradigms" are a more limited example), they and the facts sustaining them as, within the said set limits, *a priori* pre-suppositions, are inescapably tautological, as incapable of proof as of disproof, in effect, of being perceived as hypothetical. It is only when the facts that a hypothesis can alone produce generate insoluble problems, that their very conformity can lead to the suspicion of there being some inadequacy in both, a suspicion that in the given still ruling terms cannot, however, find workable expression. Only then can the supposition even begin to be entertained that there may be more than the reality (and actuality) to which these give rise, a "more" that, as going beyond the sum of (possible) facts, can, however, be neither perceived, experienced, or known, but can take only a suppositious, most often unfruitful, problematic form, always but semblance. In the world of fact the "more than fact" can assert itself only as the presence of something that the facts cannot account for. The very attempt to account for it involves self-contradiction, is self-defeating, in that the translation of the more into the form of fact, i.e., in terms of the facts existing (the only possible procedure so long as the hypothesis itself remain as the absolutely limiting factor), its attempted reception into a reality the inadequateness of which it, as the "more", expresses, denies it to be such a "more". No comprehensive, basic hypothesis can ever itself manifest in what its basal want consists, since the first requirement thereto, precisely the perception of its hypothetical nature, it itself rules out. All its unsatisfactoriness can achieve is to impel to the suspicion that it is, despite appearances, wanting, i.e., hypothetical. But in the yet ruling given terms, such a suspicion results in an impasse, for even should it take the form of a supposition that it is the (now presumed) existing hypothesis itself that constitutes the fundamental problem, there would be nothing at all by means of which it could be put to the test in that form, there being, so far, no basic standpoint radically different from the existing one that would enable such a critical examination to be undertaken. It is only a new basic hypothesis spontaneously arisen that can give the old the objective form of hypothesis needed to allow it to be perceived, experienced, cognised as such, viz., as having inherent limitations that constitute its shortcomings precisely in its nature of hypothesis merely.

A radically new hypothesis of the kind here in question is, from the standpoint of the reality and actuality shaped by the existing hypothesis, an aberration, an absurdity, which is why it can arise only spontaneously, in defiance of given facts, given reality and actuality, of perception, experience, and knowledge, reason and understanding as thereby determined and limited. The pertinence of Machado's remarks quoted as an epigraph is strikingly evidenced here: the attempt to assess the validity of the radically new hypothesis in terms that belong to the old, existing, and inadequate one, is self-evidently self-defeating. All that results, and can result, is a re-affirmation of the fact that in such terms the radically new hypothesis is without foundation, untenable, etc.

As for this new hypothesis, at its first formulation (whatever the manner in which this be done), all it can do is to assert itself as basically different, and assert at the same time that, in accord with its basic difference from the existing one (a difference in the nature of the matter hardly ever wholly grasped to begin with), the possibility is given of producing new facts, a new reality and actuality in terms of itself as generative principle, which possibility (even in favourable circumstances) can be only gradually given effect, owing to the inevitable difficulty of meeting the requirements thereto that *a fortiori* include acceptance of, and capacity for, a new objectivity, a new way of perceiving, experiencing, thinking, unlikely to be within the grasp of most of those moulded by the old hypothesis in course of being displaced. Of course, the possibility exists that the verdict of the existing hypothesis is correct, that the new, radically different one is in fact an absurdity that cannot be productively developed.

A new hypothesis (given that it be valid) need not disprove the old or its facts; nor need it solve the problems these gave rise to. It may dismiss them as the form and content of, from its radically different standpoint, a reality and actuality misproduced, misperceived, misconceived; and gradually replace them with its own facts, perceptions, conceptions, producing reality, actuality, anew as one in which the erstwhile intractable "more" can in some fashion become determined to objectivity, made accordingly perceivable, knowable, and capable of being experienced. This notwithstanding, the new reality and actuality, for all that it may fancy itself to be so, is neither more "comprehensive", nor more "true", than the one it displaces, there being nothing that might serve as a common basis for such a comparative evaluation. Every reality that has been produced as actual is, in the terms set by the basic, all-encompassing hypothesis informing it, exhaustive. It is, in the said terms that are the only available ones so long as it endures, comprehensive and true. But for this, no insoluble problems could ever arise within it in virtue of the hypothesis itself. Between it and another which it replaces, or which replaces it, there is no point of contact at all, for all that some facts appear shared, an appearance that shows itself delusive, so soon as the fundamental differences brought about by the several hypotheses are seen necessarily to affect the entirety of their respectively constituted worlds, all the facts severally contained in them. The concept of development, the intrinsic teleological nature of which (as already said) altogether excludes *generatio aequivoca*, can in no way be associated with the shift from one such hypothesis to another that can come about precisely in this spontaneous fashion alone. In the nature of the matter, such a shift can absolutely not be foreseen; nor can it, retrospectively, be represented, other than in the very manner, as a development, that is inapplicable, one that can never result in knowledge. It is always semblance, the apparent rationality of which (in the form of categories, supposed laws) is wholly illusory, however plausible in appearance. This is not to dismiss it as worthless. Speculation has its uses in suggesting possibilities beyond what reason has conceived, that may turn out to be amenable to rational investigation and prove fruitful, capable, that is, of being produced in objective, objectified form. But speculation, grandiose and far-reaching as it may seem, is not knowledge, and mistaken for it, a source only of error and confusion.

The distinction between knowledge and semblance resides wholly in one decisive character of their respective productions, the mode of which is in general otherwise identical, an identity that, failing critical examination, easily masks the difference. As with any other production, the teleological nature of production as semblance requires that the result be the starting point. No result, however, is ever given. It is always the manifestation of some intention which establishes it as the end. Such a determination is of its nature arbitrary, an arbitrariness that affects the proposed end not only in its form (as simply the decision that it shall so constitute the end), but also in its content (as what is prescribes as the *modus operandi* of its production). Here the difference between these productions comes into the open.

Within the several given limits set by society as all-encompassing hypothesis, by the prevailing "paradigmatic" hypothesis peculiar to the field in question, discussion of the various effects of which is not relevant here, what distinguishes the production that issues into knowledge, scientific production , is that it is actually carried out. It is alone owing to this actuality, to the fact that all the factors of production (agent and material, capacity and procedure) are thereby necessarily given objective, objectified existence, and, as such, have a, so to say, will and needs of their own, submission to the accordingly objective and objectified demands of which is the condition of that production; it is alone owing to this that the reciprocal correction of end and means, their testing, becomes possible, or that their irremediable falsity can be shown. The circularity of the teleological process is here to begin with clearly tentative. It is a suggestion in the form of an initially imputed productive movement among similarly imputed factors, all deduced from an at first equally arbitrarily conceived end, a suggestion tested by the operations actually undertaken with these factors to establish in what they severally properly consist, if at all, the arbitrariness vanishing (should end, material, agent, capacities, and procedure all answer) in the determination of these as lawful or rational, as definitively established (reproducible) causality. This actual pattern, that is, is not given *a priori* (other than as a causal process, an abstraction that in no way pre-determines what the needed causes and effects shall be or their precise enchainment), but determined solely by trial and error, by empirical investigation.

Semblance can ape every aspect of production, be it causality, finite teleology, empirical procedure (Toynbee, for instance, repeatedly asserts his method to be empirical), forms *in abstracto* compatible with any hypothesis and its facts, a circumstance giving it an air of actuality that masks its nature of semblance. The appeal to these formalities can, therefore, never decide whether a production be in fact actual. It is actuality itself that alone can do so, by showing the production in question to be capable of being carried out as an objective, objectified procedure in the manner just described, one in which all factors have the independent existence that enables them to assert their proper needs, those arrived at in the course of their mutual determination, mutual testing, and correction. Where this cannot be done, any seeming determination of what constitutes the (causal) rationality of a procedure, i.e., of the end and hypothesis of which it is the productive mode, empirical as it may be depicted as being, remains in effect irremediably arbitrary, as is its representation in such terms, an arbitrariness that necessarily extends to what in such a context counts as fact. Infinite teleology is clearly a hypothesis so inherently arbitrary, it being *sui generis* incapable of being given the actual objective, objectified existence (actuality) required to determine of its rationality, in that all actual (particular) production must *ex hypothesi* be for it but a manifestation of the single absolute form of process, of productive procedure, it itself sets forth in exemplary fashion.

Capital as social theory, the representation of modern society as a particular instance of infinite teleology, thus falls squarely into the category of semblance, together with its facts, so far as these arise out of the hypothesis itself, that informs the representation.

It may be proper to suppose that present society must, like all others hitherto, die away. The supposition, even if it were correct, however, does not, and cannot, count as knowledge, there being no possible manner in which such a progression can be given actual determinate causal form in advance of its completion (assuming such completion to come about). Indeed, were knowledge of this available, it would involve contradiction, since it would *eo ipso* constitute the means of preventing what as unknown and unknowable must be accounted a fatality. This knowledge would manifest the fact that society had been brought within the compass of lawful (controlled) production, finite teleology, one to which a representation as infinite teleology (as fatality) would then be absurd and irrelevant. Whether correct or not, the supposition, in the wholly indeterminate form in which present knowledge and experience at least, alone allow it to be expressed, is consequently wholly useless, though some of its speculative consequences may prove to be fruitful.

The development set forth by Marx purports to be cognition going beyond this that may serve as a guide to revolutionary praxis. This, in the nature of teleology, finite or infinite, is impossible. Whether as actual causality, or its semblance, a teleologically determined procedure can have only one result: the production of the specific end in terms of which this determination comes about in the course of the matching specific procedure required thereto, one that *a priori* excludes the production of any other end in the given terms (if, that is, the end and procedure have been correctly determined). The metaphor of the womb used by Marx disallows his purpose in so doing. What is produced *ex utero* is generically the same as that which produces, such differences as there may be being but of subordinate significance. Were a dog to give birth to a cat, the circumstance would be as remarkable as that present society could result, in Marx's fashion, in a radically different one. The alternative imposes itself: if Marx be describing present society, the result he proposes cannot be derived from it; or, if the result be what he asserts it to be, he cannot be describing present society as the mode of its genesis. This dilemma of *Capital* as social theory, that derives from the determination of revolution as end, cannot be resolved; or rather, its resolution lies in the exhibition of the inadmissibility of that determination, which demolishes the theory.

The determination of revolution as end involves consciousness as the decisive factor, which gives the process the purposiveness necessary to it as one of production. That Marx should have been guarded and sparing in his remarks about the radically new society to be brought about does not alter the fact that he must have envisaged it in essential respects, if the conception of its realisation as a production process taking place within present society was to be at all possible. In the nature of consciousness as wholly reflexive this is impossible. Given the absolute limit set to the possibility of perception, knowledge, and experience by the all-encompassing hypothesis that informs a society as its necessarily uncognised and uncognisable pre-supposition, consciousness in all its manifestations can never be other than conventional, indeed, poriomanic. Even its most fanciful, imaginative representations are inescapably but the combination of re-cognisable elements, viz., elements the cognition of which has been so and in no other way constituted and established in the course of whatever production society as hypothesis about man and Nature at any time gives rise to.

The radically new can thus never be produced, for which reason we are forced to describe its generation as spontaneous, i.e., as to us non-rational, unlawful, a description having reference not to that to which it is applied, since we know, and can know, nothing about its manner of coming to be, but to our ignorance concerning this, to the fact that its production is beyond our capacity and means. This being so, radical social change, whether for good or ill, not only is beyond being envisaged in any terms (the expression itself being but a wholly indeterminate abstraction to which no sense at all can be attached, other than it is in some inconceivable manner fundamentally different from what actually exists); but moreover, were it to take place, could not initially be perceived and known to have done so, the new forms in terms of which the consciousness of its having done so could alone come about, not having yet been produced sufficient to that end.

This Marx's social theory denies, as does all social theory deriving from it which so far as it departs from the pattern originally set down (most strikingly in recent times, Joseph Weber's *The Great Utopia*), does so only in such respects as do not affect the basic premise. However, the critical stance needed to cognise the limits of present society as all-encompassing hypothesis that Marx assumed, and had of its very nature to assume, himself to have, is *a priori* ruled out by those very limits, that very hypothesis. The distinction between bourgeois and socialist consciousness as respectively false and true, crucial to Marx's social theory, has no validity. Social consciousness can never be, or yield, anything other than semblance, be, in Marx's terms, false, whatever the manner of its representation, in that it (as said) necessarily must take for granted as its informing presupposition that, the cognition of which alone, could enable it to become knowledge, make it actually critical. Marx's social theory is (like all essays at a comprehensive explanation of society) a wholly speculative construction, a circumstance that makes the numberless attempts to bring it into line with fatality wasted labour. The idea underlying these attempts, that fatality has falsified the theory in this or that respect which so far needs, and can be given correction, is a misconception arising from the failure to grasp the theory as semblance and understand what this involves.

Semblance, to repeat, is what is represented by the illicit extension of reason to that which has not been, or cannot be, produced. The standpoint of semblance, as an apparent finite teleological process (albeit that, as in Marxism, it is but a particular form of process in general), but for which its representation would not be possible, necessarily requires an assumption of the end that, as unavoidably a pre-determination, is *sui generis* unwarrantable. Semblance has, and can have, no objective, objectified, existence, no actuality independent of its representation by which it could be tested. Representation in the form of semblance is by its nature thus caught in a vicious circle: the facts adduced in its support are themselves produced by the pseudo-rational (causal) process it presupposes, i.e., imputes to that which but for this could otherwise not even be given the appearance of having been made apprehensible and comprehensible. The idea that fatality falsifies some form of semblance in one or other respect necessarily involves a *petitio principi*, since only in terms of its given representation, as having the general features imputed to it as a causal process, can the supposition be entertained. That, for instance, there have been revolutions—attempts at radically changing present society—that have failed is a supposition possible only given their prior representation *a priori* as the end of social processes, which itself depicts these events, these processes, in such fashion as accords with that end. Or again, that the working class is no longer the carrier of radical (revolutionary) change is an assertion based on the assumption of its having been so in the first place, that holds good only within a representation of social processes that stipulates this to be its role in accordance with the imputed causality that itself determines these to be the social processes. The idea of falsification is, in effect, in relation to fatality, a self-contradiction, in that if the causal processes were in general what semblance represents it to be, if, that is, fatality were at all capable of being actually exhibited as a causal process, it would be abolished *qua* fatality.

In sum, semblance as but make-believe production (so far as its relation to actuality is concerned) has, and can have, only accordant make-believe relations to fatality which it in reality cannot affect in any respect of consequence. It being wholly self-enclosed, its informing categories (whatever these may be conceived as being in any general social theory) are, taken as reflected, *idola theatri*. Semblance is thus inescapably dogmatic, the more so, the more systematically articulated. Yet it is essential, since but for some pseudo-rational representation of what otherwise would be sheer fortuity, be it but the assumption that the future will in basal respects be like the past as it is conceived to have been, life would become utterly senseless and impossible. The rejection of one form of semblance in terms of another, little as this may be allowed by those who suppose themselves to be merely reflecting what is so, without the intervention of what to them is *a priori* tendentious theory, achieves only a substitution of identicals that in itself contributes nothing to knowledge. It is not only social theory that falls into the sphere of semblance. Any theory does so, so far as it goes beyond what can be actually produced, and postulates elements and relations that cannot be given objective, objectified (actual, independent) existence, that are but speculative suppositions demanded by the theory. This is to say: any radically different hypothesis must *ipso facto* appear to the present one as just such a dogmatic absurdity going beyond any possible conceivable facts, viz., as semblance, and is so, to the extent that the facts it proposes in principle have not been, or cannot be, produced as actual.

From the standpoint of semblance the concept of ideology falls away. The distinction between alleged false consciousness (one unaware of its presuppositions and thus at bottom always uncritical, appearances notwithstanding) and true, from which it derives is grounded in the reflection theory. Only on such a theory, one blind to the fact that it makes its own initial projections the test of its categories, can objectivity be supposed in any way to involve the correspondence of what is produced, with that unwarrantably presumed to be known as pre-existing in that form and content independently of that production, the supposed possibility of agreement functioning as the means of verifying, of proving, the product to be objectively true. In the nature of production, however, a concept and its objective embodiment, its actuality (where achieved), are one, i.e., necessarily correspond in essential respects at least, since the actuality of anything is, and can be, nothing but the objective, objectified, the pro-duced concept now independently existing as a re-cognisable thing. That the world, so far as we know, and can only know it, is objectively true means no more than that we re-cognise it to be what it is only in virtue of the fact that it is nothing but the produced embodiment of our cognition. Such truth is not (as the reflection theory holds) a test or proof of the correctness of this cognition in the sense of measuring up to something other than it, our knowledge being wholly enclosed within, wholly con-fined to it, it being itself the absolute bar to our ever being able to have any yardstick independent of it. The resulting circumstance, that with respect both to form and content, we know and can know only what we produce as we produce it, that we have no means whatever of knowing what the world is like other than this (for all that, in the nature of production as productive of first Nature simultaneously with second, we are forced to conclude that the world as we know it is not all there is), transforms truth in the sense required by correspondence, verification, into circular agreement that reduces to nullity. Relative to theory, to the general hypotheses we form in any field in order to grasp, to produce the world as a rational, causal process so far as it falls within its terms, the principle of verification, insofar as it requires an independent actuality as one of its terms, shows itself to be untenable, since this presupposes knowledge independent of what we alone can have, can produce, for ourselves. Verification here reveals itself as necessarily grounded in dogma, as involving always a *petitio principi* that deprives it of validity: it is always evidence of the uncritical acceptance of some semblance taken to be actual. The distinction drawn between what is and what is not ideological that depends upon verification for warranty is no more than the consequence of such an acceptance, an aspect of the polemical strug-gle of one semblance with another, or others. As such it has no critical function at all, the criticism of one dogma by another being itself dog-matic, not just without, but owing to its very point of departure without any possibility of ever attaining to, scientific validity as knowledge.

In its concern with presuppositions, the concept of ideology nonethe-less points to a circumstance, but for the grasp of which there can be no understanding of the nature, limits, and function of critique. It is that production itself (and *a fortiori* the perception, knowledge, and experience directly and indirectly associated with it, perception, know-ledge, and experience as such, that is) may be said to be "ideological". This is so, because its objectivity, its objectifications, viz., the actuality of its results, are necessarily partial, one-sided, owing to the manner of their coming-to-be as that which inescapably is accompanied by unknowable residues (what I have called "first Nature"). The omnipresence of this partiality, this one-sidedness, allied to the fact that it can never be more than asserted to be, there being in the nature of its coming about no possible way of our ever knowing in what it consists, easily leads to its being overlooked. Yet it is this necessarily wholly empty abstraction that provides the only available ground for a rational critique of society, in that it allows of the idea that production and its accompanying perception, knowledge, and experience (together with the semblance that also is produced within the given limits) constitute only a hypothesis about the nature of the world, of society, man, and Nature.

The objection that, since we cannot in any way give this hypothesis actuality so that we might know it for what it is, its limits (there being for us nothing that could be used for the purpose, the given production, knowledge, perception, experience, as also semblance—all we have and can have—being informed by it as their presupposition), it is of no prac-tical or theoretical significance neglects the crucial point. This is that as but a hypothesis, it does not (anymore than did previous hypotheses of this kind) say the last word about society, man, and Nature, which could be other than they are for us, as presently constituted in accordance with its presuppositions unknowable to us. In other words, the limits it sets to the possibility of perception, knowledge, and experience, of theory and practice, with respect to itself are absolute only for us, and only for so long as society, homo faber nature and second Nature, that is, remains as that hypothesis has constituted it to be. Such a concept removes the last refuge of dogma, the belief that present society is the Absolute Idea of society incarnate (so far as this can be), while at the same time avoiding the equally dogmatic error involved in prejudging what some radically new society, some radically new hypothesis, might be. That, as said, the ration-ality of critique stems from its making this impractical, wholly abstract general concept of the hypothetical nature of society and the world belonging to it, and it alone, its point of departure becomes manifest in the circumstance that only from it is it possible to conclude that social theory is not knowledge but semblance, illusion, and to show why this must be so. The function of critique is not to dispel such illusion, but to elucidate the fact that this is impossible, i.e., to dispel the illusion that it could ever be other than merely the illusion of knowledge.

Critique cannot issue in practical recommendations. In terms of its very standpoint, it must take as given that it itself is informed by the very lim-its which it shows to be comprehensively at work. Indeed, the demand for practical recommendations as the index of the worth of a theory that deals with society in some fashion is, as Wilde long since pointed out, always grounded in acceptance of the given society as in essential respect "in harmony with the Notion of society," that denies the very possibility of critique. For the general goal of critique, to which it is driven by the perception of what appears to be some fundamental malfunction in society that resists all attempts to set it right, is necessarily restricted to showing that, if it be real, the malfunction is intrinsic to the very unknowable limits of society inherent in it as but a specific, one-sided, hypothesis; that it is a malfunction not in, but of, society, of a nature accordingly unknowable to us for what it actually may be, i.e., as other than in some or other illusory fashion excogitated in the course of attempts to overcome it, attempts thus in themselves self-defeating, in that they and the malfunction necessarily have, and must have, a common basis that is *a priori* unknowable. Further than this critique cannot go without destroying its foundations, either as the then assumption that society is not hypothetical but definitively true, and that this truth is knowable to us; or the assumption that though existing society is hypothetical, the hypothesis is knowable, and in terms of its perceived, cognised limits, provides itself the means for the (conscious) production of another, radically different one.

If, from the standpoint of critique, it is immaterial, relative to the understanding of the matter, what semblance (illusion) one choose, or merely accept unaware of its illusory nature, it is otherwise in practical life. For semblance here is itself no eidolon, but an effective power that acts as a determinant of individual and collective life, precisely owing to the fact that it is the only means whereby society in general can be given the necessary appearance of rationality, of having the (causal) lawfulness indispensable to purposive activity, an appearance which, although imputed, is with equal necessity taken to be not appearance, but reflection of what actually exists, independently of our having so structured it, to which we must subordinate ourselves, if our purposes are to be so determined as to have the possibility of being achieved. Such an appearance functions more or less adequately, when it does so, only by permission, so to say, of the essential fatality that removes society as a whole from the sphere of lawfulness. This unlawfulness, which Marx conceived as the anarchy of production in its universal aspect, plainly does not derive, as he mistakenly supposed it to, from commodity production, however this may affect its particular form of manifestation; but has, heretofore at least, always prevailed, as the breakdown of all previous societies witnesses.

The revelation of the inescapability of illusion (semblance) relative to society and its world, resulting from the circumstance that society as a whole has demonstrably not in actuality been brought within the confines of finite teleology, of causally lawful production, elucidates the following. Since, but for some such speculative representation of society in seemingly rational (causal) terms, one that necessarily appertains to the given produced second Nature and accordant homo faber nature, organised (purposive) social life would be wholly impossible, it ensues that any organisation, any purpose, what we conceive to be the end of society, of existence, viz., the very categories we use to define them, however we do so, and the human nature that fittingly belongs with them, are themselves forms of semblance. In that these taken together are the only categories we have, and can have (the given second Nature and homo faber nature exhausting all possibilities open to us), categories but for which no such representation of any kind would be possible, it further ensues that the most ideal representations of society and human nature we can frame can never be other than abstract embodiments of existing society and human nature, "purged" of what, in terms of whatever dogmatic presupposition be at work, appears inessential dross. Such embodiments compound their illusory nature of semblance in that they involve the assumption that these mere abstractions could in principle have actuality, and that were they to have it, they would constitute something radically different from the presently existing that is their ground. The intolerance that so frequently accompanies attempts to put ideals into practice stems from this, from the fact that the supposed "dross" is in actuality integral to that of which the ideals are but abstractions, incapable of ever being given effect in such "pure" form, that makes demands going against the "human nature" from which they derive, demands that require sacrifices that appear, and indeed are, unjust and so only exceptionally freely made.

In reality, all the categories that inform social theory concerned with understanding and removing the injustices of society have just this illusory nature of ideals (and are in that sense themselves ideal) in that they all inescapably carry forward the injustice that impelled to their conception as the means of overcoming it, and reproduce it, even if not in its exact original form. The reason is not that they are incorrectly framed, that other, more adequate, categories would in principle be available, if only we could reach a better understanding. It is that the attempt to grasp in what the injustice consists constitutes a contradiction in terms. As earlier argued, in finite teleology, purposive productive activity, the purpose to be achieved, as directing power, necessarily requires the strict subordination to itself of material and agent which exist for it only in the specific form and content appropriate to itself, all else, whatever it may be, being not simply irrelevant, but, if it intrude, an obstacle to successful realisation, and so needing to be suppressed. To be at all, that is, production must needs involve injustice, in that material and agent are always more than, and different from, what it compulsorily restricts them to be, as which they themselves have been produced (exception having to be made for completely artificial materials and agents which, with respect to their second Nature actuality, are just what they have been produced to be). The injustice is transmitted, as both cause and effect, to the results of production, in general, second nature and homo faber. Since knowledge comes about only in, and through, production, as do perception and experience, as reflection of and on that which has been produced as actually, objectively existing, viz., in the objective, objectified form (and content) of an independent object, as which alone it can be known, perceived, experienced, it follows that our very knowledge, perception, experience are themselves grounded in injustice, but for which they would not be possible. In other words, our very concept of Nature and man in the form and with the content in which they are alone cognisable (as presently produced second Nature and homo faber nature) is informed by the injustice their production presupposes, which it takes, and must take, for granted as "in the nature of things."

The description of this inherent aspect of production as "injustice" is not an actual determination, but an abstraction logically entailed by the supposition deriving from the nature of production itself that there is more to Nature and man than their produced form of second Nature and homo faber nature, more to life than the struggle for survival, a supposition, as shown earlier, likewise without any possible conceivable content.

In determinate form and content, injustice is always a product of accidental historical circumstances out of which its opposite likewise arises as a related definite idea, whether practicable or not. That such modes of injustice may be remediable (namely, that the justice that is the ideal expression of their defects can in some fashion be realised in actuality) gives rise to the idea that injustice itself is an historical, accidental, and so revocable, condition. This is not so. As an irremovable determining condition of production and its results, injustice itself is a fatality. Being primary, injustice is the inescapable ground for any possible kind of justice, constitutes its limit in being a fundamental feature of the struggle for survival (individual and collective), and needs must enter into its very determination as part of its content, making the concept and actuality of justice (that always relates to, and arises out of, some specific historical mode of injustice), of its nature relative, partial, and if carried beyond its proper measure, self-contradictory, i.e., the injustice that is its ground then asserts itself once more. (And similarly with right, tolerance, and all categories of this kind.)

Try as we may, we are thus constrained, in theory and practice, i.e., in all conceivable circumstances, to remain within the limits set by injustice, compulsion, wrong as inherent aspects of human existence, so far as it is determined by the struggle for survival, in that it is wholly impossible to produce (and so to conceive of) the conditions from which they would be absent. Any determination we can give them can only be speculative, a form of semblance that begs the question and makes the attempt to remove the injustice, etc., deriving from such a determination self-defeating.

The conventional view takes this for granted, since for it the struggle for survival is the lot of "man", and must ever be the generally determining and limiting factor in human existence. It follows that the utmost that can be done is to determine the mean between excess and defect, namely, to reduce injustice, compulsion, wrong, etc., to that minimal quantum unavoidable in practical life, something even so hardly achievable in actuality, the obstacles to its being so, being virtually insurmountable, "human nature" being what it is.

The impossibility of doing more is shown by Kant's attempts to ground morality in general and necessary principles. The attempt involves a sleight of hand: the representation as deduction of what has been, and can have been, arrived at only inductively, i.e., in a manner that inherently prevents the result from having the one character demanded by, and of, the required principles, that of necessity. Were Kant's moral principles to be what he wished them to be, it would be practical morality only that would be a *pis aller*, being no more than a compromise with the injustice, compulsion, wrong, etc., inescapable in daily life. That is to say, such compromise with injustice, compulsion, wrong, etc., would, on this showing, be a historical, revocable, requirement such that, at least in principle, it would be possible to imagine circumstances in which it would no longer be needed. But just this is what is impossible, in that injustice, compulsion, wrong, etc., are, as shown, the first and intrinsic elements of morality. "Metaphysical" principles of morality as Kant would have them, if properly thought out in terms of the nature of morality such as it arises from, and as part of, the struggle for survival, would necessarily result in showing their own impossibility, to be to the extent that injustice, compulsion, wrong, etc., are fundamental aspects of morality, unavoidably at once also metaphysical principles of immorality.

Nonetheless, Kant's view must remain the starting point of any reconsideration of moral theory, just because of its critical suggestion that, were circumstances and man other than they are, the present *pis aller* would no longer be needed, except, for reasons to be discussed, within a restricted sphere. For him, in the then given conditions, this possibility could never be more than an idea. The analysis of production here undertaken radically alters this, suggesting that the limits of perception, knowledge, and experience are not merely other than what Kant took them to be, but that, even in this different form, they are absolute only for man as homo faber. The possibility mentioned then ceases to be in perpetuity but an idea, or rather, it is so only for homo faber. It becomes reasonable to suppose that there are, albeit only in principle, possible actual conditions that would permit that which is more than homo faber (and more than second Nature) to find expression. Since, however, such conditions must, as already stated, be beyond production, nothing whatsoever can be foreknown about them, or about the manner in which, if at all, they might come about.

It follows that the conventional view, and Kant's in practice, are not wrong, other than in being without limit. So far as homo faber and second

Nature, i.e., production, the struggle for survival, remain absolutely necessary to human existence, to that extent must injustice, compulsion, wrong, etc., remain fundamental conditions of life, and justice, right, etc., manifest themselves as grounded in, and limited (determined) by, their opposites that belong in the nature of production, of the struggle for survival, themselves. This is so not merely of social relations. The fact that the human nature of homo faber must, to whatever extent it may be, necessarily also remain, means that the injustice, compulsion, wrong, etc., that inform it must to that extent remain determinants of individual relations. It is tempting to suppose that, since they pertain to homo faber nature, such relations will not be unlike those we know and experience today in many respects. But such a supposition is unwarrantable. As noted, a radically new hypothesis necessarily alters everything related to it in concomitant radical fashion. It itself being, *qua* radically new, not knowable to us in any way whatsoever, so likewise must the form and content of everything that belongs to it in suitably changed incarnation.

Kant, however, is correct in this, that for all that it has become possible to suppose that the conditions required for life beyond the limitations of homo faber could in principle be established, it is absolutely impossible to have any conception of what they would be like in actuality, an impossibility that arises out of the very nature of conception itself as presently produced. What is more than, and radically different from, homo faber, lies beyond the compass of finite teleology, in which cognition as we know, and can only know it, arises. Present thought can go no further than to describe this as spontaneity, a description of its nature without any possible content, that asserts simply the fact that this, whatever it may be, cannot be known in the only terms presently available to us, at least.

If it is to be rescued, the critical aspect of Kant's conception must be recast in accordance with that conception's transformation in terms of the idea of homo faber and second Nature. From the fact that injustice, compulsion, wrong, etc., as such, are fundamental to production, to the struggle for survival, it follows, as just argued, that the relativity of their accidental historical manifestations and related opposites is not just the effect of the limit of all possible knowledge and experience in Kant's sense, i.e., only for us; but is theirs in actuality, it being impossible to produce them in any other way. That being so, it becomes inadmissible to suppose justice, right, etc., to have "in themselves" a different form and content that would enable them in this different fashion to be features of a mode of life beyond production, a supposition that flows from the mistaken view that injustice, compulsion, wrong, etc., as such stem not from the very nature of production, but from some or other of its particular modes characterised in their several ways by class division which, once overcome, would leave justice, right, etc., as a realised content, a justice, right, etc., absolute. The hypostatis therein involved is characteristic of semblance. In actuality, justice, right, etc., like their several grounds, injustice, compulsion, wrong, etc., are strictly production relations, or what is the same, social relations. Of what lies beyond production we can say nothing, other than that those relations which production *sui generis* generates and establishes (in whatever may be their varied historical accidental forms) must necessarily be absent from it. It falls to critique to show these and other categories to be relations of this kind, insofar as they are susceptible of actual determination, i.e., to show that, as other than as so determined, as other than these, all determinations of this kind are, and can be, but semblance.

V

To ascertain this with respect to categories like justice, right, etc., that appear inherently problematical is perhaps less difficult than it is with respect to others that appear self-evident, straightforward, empirically establishable matters of fact. "Waste" is a conspicuous example of these, allied to which are "conservation", so-called "alternative" and "intermediate" technology and associated ideas held to embody in germ requirements essential to overcoming the malfunction of present society, in effect, to a radical restructuring of present society.

"Waste" here is used in an absolute sense. The supposition that production for exchange of its nature results in production that can be correctly termed "superfluous" is found already in Marx (*Grundrisse*). In modern times, it has found clearest expression in Joseph Weber's concept of "abstract production," production which, though necessary to the needs of systematic exchange (profit) as determined by universal competition, is of no conceivable use relative to the satisfaction of human needs (or of those of "Nature" from the standpoint of conservation as presently conceived). It is thus absolute waste, of which arms production and those kinds of production that (so far as present knowledge goes) irreparably harm the environment in respect of its capacity to sustain life, are taken as self-evident forms, and proof of the correctness of the concept.

Critically considered, however, the concept itself shows the circularity that nullifies the supposed proof, in that it, sc. the determination of absolute waste, is not, indeed cannot be, derived from existing production. In the context of this production, "waste" is capable of objective determination only in qualified fashion, when considered from a particular standpoint. As such, "waste" of any kind (even should it take the form of apparently sheer destruction of material and agent) has a productive function, and is a category, a relation of production. Not being a relation of this kind, "absolute waste" is thus semblance. It is, in effect, a (moral) judgment upon some kinds of production, or, more generally, upon production as a whole in its given form, deriving from some fanciful (supposedly radically different) conception of society and human needs, about which, in this connection, nothing can be said that would not be tediously repetitive.

There are, however, other assumptions at work here that will repay examination. The chief concerns production. The dismissal of certain kinds of production as absolute waste does not, of course, extend to those of their results that are manifestly useful, for instance, those that in practice or in principle reduce or wholly do away with toilsome labour. What is assumed is that, had production been carried on in some presumed radically different manner—had it been "for use" instead of "for exchange"—the same results would have been achieved by design, instead of, as now frequently, by chance, i.e., without the alleged absolute waste of which these results are but a side effect, the production in question having other ends in view. But on this very premise the assumption is untenable, since that very radical difference in modes of production (which here is accepted as such for the sake of the argument) would make it impossible in given circumstances to foreknow what, in such wholly altered conditions, would, or could, be produced. Given, however, that the asserted difference in modes of production is, as has been before argued, an error, the assumption that there was (and is) in principle some other manner of achieving these desirable results is once more wholly without foundation, though for different reasons. In short, but for the alleged absolute waste production, viz., but for the fact that production is carried on as it is, the results in question would never have come about at all; or, perhaps better, there is no knowing whether they would, or could, have done so, and certainly no grounds for asserting definitively that they would, or could. The error underlying the belief that this is not so stems from a failure to grasp the nature of finite teleology on the one hand, and to appreciate the essential role of accidentality in its several forms relative to production on the other.

As an objective, objectified, actually determined process, production is carried out strictly in accordance with the rules (or laws) that express the requirements of the purpose to be realised, with respect to all factors involved. From it, accident has (so far as possible) been removed in the course of the prior trial and error needed to establish what exactly these requirements are that will make the result answer to the purpose, i.e., make the process a finite teleological one. Finite teleology is the sphere of settled patterned repetition, of planned activity. Were accident, of which spontaneity could be considered an instance, wholly to be prevented, innovation (though perhaps not improvement of existing procedures) would be excluded. It follows that were production as a whole in the entirety of its relations, viz., society, definitively brought within the confines of such teleology, accidentality, and with it radical change, would no longer be possible (other than that brought about by what, in terms of the very mechanism of production, is inherently beyond all possibility of being produced, can come about only as a fatality of its nature absolutely incomprehensible to us, that, that is, that occurs in first Nature). It would no longer be possible not only in general, but in particular, in respect of any aspect of production, a change in which would materially affect fundamental relations. A planned society, were it possible, would be one from which all but inconsequential change had been ruled out. Now such a society is presumed to result from so-called production for use, a mode of production that allegedly puts an end to the anarchy, the accidentality, asserted to be characteristic only of production for exchange. The supposition that results first obtained by accident, owing either to some unforeseen and unforeseeable malfunction of the productive process, or to some equally unforeseen and unforeseeable chance application in other areas of production, results the effect of which is to change production relations decisively, because of their radical, innovative character, could as well have been obtained by design in conditions that expressly rule out such change, is thus patently absurd.

It is so in another respect. What comes about by accident cannot be foreknown. No prior conception of it is, in the nature of the matter, possible. Only as having happened (initially, to us, spontaneously) does it, whatever it may be, become conceivable at all, capable in principle of becoming an object of knowledge, of being given actual objective, objectified determination, of being produced. (The seemingly contradictory aphorism, "chance favours the prepared mind," relates to quite different circumstances. It relates to theoretically conceived possibilities that first become even in principle determinable in actuality, only owing to their having been hypothetically conceived, the theory directing attention to the detection of their occurrence which would otherwise not have been capable of being so noticed, strictly, to their production in this then objectifiable determinate form and content, as which they then may be able to be produced actually to exist.) But prior conception is essential to finite teleological process, as the idea of its determining purposed end, that alone enables the production to be planned, to come about by design. The supposition here in question must thus assume as achieved that which it asserts production for use would have resulted in without such pre-achievement, a manifest contradiction.

Relative to production as such, accident in general arises from one or other of two causes: either from defective knowledge, when it may be said to be internal to the production process; or from the fact that production is inherently competitive, when it may be said to be external to the process of production, to determine these relations that arise in the course of that competition (and their possibility and possible range), relations that themselves give production its decisive impulse at any time, namely, to determine what, within the possibilities open to given knowledge, production shall in the main be concerned with. In their interrelations, the two modes extend and reinforce each other. Accident resulting from defective knowledge develops knowledge in ways necessarily unforeseen and unforeseeable, that open new possibilities for production, altering the means with which the struggle for survival (competition) can be carried on. This in turn allows the accidentality of that struggle to manifest itself in new forms, to give rise to new relations that then work back on production, giving it a general direction that accords with these new forms and relations. (This is so of production in general; but the same holds for more limited fields.) The consequent impulse to exploitation of these new productive possibilities then sets the stage for the intrusion of new accidents arising from defective knowledge, and so forth. In the nature of this inescapable concatenation of accidents, it is (whatever may be the requirements of production as such considered theoretically as a finite teleological process) *a priori* impossible in practice to predetermine, to foreknow, to plan, production or knowledge in their entirety, as a development, give them the form of a perfectly achieved rational, finite teleological process. The illusion or semblance of such rationality arises *a tergo*, as a reflection upon what has been achieved, which can be represented (but only retrospectively) as a development come about owing to the workings of some immanent necessity (what Hegel conceived to be the "inner logic" of the process), of which the apparent accidentality is then asserted to be but the phenomenal form. Only if such a representation be taken as a prospectively achievable actuality, instead of being accepted as an illusion excogitated with hindsight on false premises, can it be supposed that were this or another necessity properly grasped, it would be possible to plan the future as a development in all essentials, so avoiding the accidentality, the waste, heretofore inevitable.

The struggle for survival, the fundamental mode of which is competition, has, however, and can have, no such rationality, nor, *a fortiori*, has, or can have, production as a whole, the (in a specific sense) peculiar human form of that struggle. All societies attempt, in one way or another, to prescribe the bounds and the forms within which the struggle is permissible, bounds and forms judged compatible with their stability, self-preservation. That is to say, they attempt to give it a rational, or lawful, form, in accordance with the general, exhaustive hypothesis about the nature of Nature and man that informs them, appears to them the nature of Nature and man as they are *sui generis*.

The idea deriving from Marx that general competition simply as such is a distinguishing feature of commodity production, correct and useful as it may be (if it be) in economic theory, is an error in social theory. In reality, competition is the basic determining relation of society itself, whatever its form, thus always general, in that society, the sum of relations established by production at any time between men and their environment and among themselves as so constituted, is but the organisation of the struggle for survival. What differs between one society and another are the forms this competition, this struggle, takes. The more extensive and varied becomes the produced world (the properties and capacities of material and agent), the more, self-evidently, do the possibilities for competition, i.e., for accidentality in the two general forms just mentioned. But the extension has no effect upon the intensity of competition. Within the given limits of a society at any time, the outcome partly of the opportunities production affords for the struggle for survival, partly of the bounds set to their exploitation by act of will, competition, accidentality, is always at full pitch. It is only historical illusion, arising from the comparison of different societies, a comparison always anachronistic (sc. invalid) owing to the fact that its basis must always be the present taken to be the result of a development in which previous societies necessarily appear only as incomplete forms of what has now first been fully realised, that yields the erroneous belief that the intensity of competition, of accidentality, was relatively less acute in earlier societies, i.e., that in them these cannot be taken to be general determinants of social life, in the way they now have to be. It is this that has, among other things, given to simple reproduction ("production for use") its seductive appearance of being *per se* more rational than expanded reproduction ("production for exchange"), an appearance that fails to distinguish what is properly rational (that which falls into the compass of finite teleology, and is no different from modern technology in this respect, however more restricted production may have been), from what is merely the outcome of the limits imposed upon the then given possibilities by productive techniques and knowledge, in general by the exhaustive hypothesis about Nature and human nature (second Nature and homo faber) informing society to which these give rise, an outcome in no way whatever the effect of rationality, of a finite teleological determination of society itself as a whole, as supposed, or rather, as assumed as the premise of this supposition.

The inherently prejudicial nature of the historical illusion of knowledge is strikingly illustrated in that past societies are necessarily viewed from the standpoint of their completion, their downfall, a perspective that inescapably to some extent informs our judgment of them, in that (*inter alia*) it suggests to retrospective consideration possibilities that, had they been seized, might have averted or deferred it. To impute reality to these possibilities in the past is to overlook the fact that they appear real only in terms not only of subsequent knowledge, i.e., in the light of that completion and the alternatives it alone can suggest as having been in principle available, but also of subsequent experience of Nature and human nature, both radically different from those then possible and obtaining. The struggle for survival of which given perception, knowledge, and experience are at any time the expression is always a struggle for the survival of Nature and human nature in the specific form and with the specific content society as exhaustive hypothesis gives, and alone can give, them in the course of its simultaneous production of itself and its environment, and is absolutely restricted to this. As actually occurring, it is of its nature blind to any possibilities not accordant with itself in this form and with this purpose, so that even should there be a presentiment of failure (which does indeed occur), and even should it subsequently be shown to have been a legitimate one, the understanding of what such failure actually consisted in is *a priori* ruled out, the very efforts to prevent it, necessarily misconceived, having an accordant effect not meet to the purpose, supposing them to have any effect at all.

This fundamental error of historical illusion is intrinsic to historical retrospection that, to make the past intelligible to the present, must begin with the definitive result as the quasi-teleological determining starting point. Prospectively, of course, given the essential accidentality of the struggle for survival, nothing can ever be so determined to be a, or the, definitive result; so that the future (other than as rational semblance needed for purposive activity) is, rationally considered, inherently unforeseeable, and so unintelligible. Prospectively, that is, things necessarily almost always look quite other, and are other, than they do, and are, to historical representation, the very premise of which, the intelligibility of the past that *eo ipso* must include what to it was the future, makes misconception, misjudgment, inevitable, however conscientiously it be attempted to avoid it. Were it possible, which it is not, to write of the present and future in the past as it appeared to it in its terms, viz., without any prejudgment whatsoever arising from what subsequently can be taken to be its necessity, all that would be achieved would be a record of chance events, and speculations about their possible significance in terms of some dogmatic presupposition, some semblance, such as is found in present-day newspapers and other writings devoted to that purpose.

With respect to the future, then, "waste", as other than a production category, i.e., as absolute, is wholly indeterminable. It has thus no place at all in social theory, so far as this remains (or attempts to remain) within the strict confines of (critical) reason. From the standpoint of such theory, the topic is exhausted in the statement that all the activities relating to the struggle for survival, to the preservation of society as at any time constituted, however they may later appear, have some definite function, for all that it may no longer be possible, from the vantage point of a radically different society, to grasp precisely what the function of some or other activity was, or even to perceive it as having any function at all. That something appears from such a vantage point a crass waste of resources absolutely considered means no more than that the activity in question, its material and agent, its purpose, no longer are a feature of the struggle for survival of society. Similarly with what appears to be the sheerest irresponsibility, the most reasonless persistence in behaviour seemingly (to later view) quite contrary to self-interest, and so on—all these are judgments possible to a hindsight that, from a radically new basis alone, can, as said, see matters in the perspective of completion, see possibilities in terms of this perspective which, at the time to which they are subsequently imputed retrospectively, did not exist, and could not have existed, in this form. That is to say, even supposing they had been capable of being perceived *in abstracto*, a supposition that must be allowed largely to stress the point, they would, and could, not have been considered practicable in the then given social terms, which comes to the same in effect.

What holds good for the future as it was to the past, holds for it as it is to the present. The presentiment of failure, collapse, doom (however one may wish to call it) that is so marked an aspect of present social life is, and can but be, wholly speculative, whatever the form in which this failure be represented, since we can have absolutely no means of foreknowing whether it be legitimate or not, as a consequence of present production and its relations.

As factual representation, the presentiment unavoidably takes the form of extrapolation. The premise of this procedure is the condition "other things being equal," i.e., the denial of the essential (internal and external) accidentality of the struggle for survival, of production This premise compels the procedure to deny what it is used to affirm: if accidentality be no longer at work, the struggle for survival must have been brought to a halt. In other words, production as a whole, in all its essential relations, society, that is, must have come within the compass of cognised, constituted necessity, and therewith of established determination, in sum, of finite teleology, a condition of its nature incompatible with a failure asserted to arise from the given production processes and procedures themselves. Moreover, if this be so of the future, considered in terms of present production, it follows that what holds for it must already be so, since the ground of the represented failure necessary to extrapolation is that production and its relations will, in general respects, henceforth be what they are now, i.e., it follows that the presentiment must assume the struggle for survival to be already halted, an assumption clearly absurd in itself, and in that it makes the very presentiment nonsensical, as either impossible, or as having already become actual.

It nonetheless remains that other than in such logically self-contradictory fashion, no factual representation of failure can be made at all, since, once essential accidentality be admitted, and therewith, be it but as possibility and probability, radically new productive processes involving just as radically new capacities and properties of material and agent, of resources, that is, the ground for it vanishes with the replacement of the production processes and relations that functioned as its point of departure. In sum, from a rational standpoint, all such factual representations, like the supposed theoretically demonstrable necessary ones, viz., these presentiments as such, are baseless, given the intrinsic unintelligibility of the future so long as it remains the outcome of the struggle for survival, and to the extent that it does so. This does not mean that, in apparent factual form, they are wholly useless in practice, however; for in that they may direct attention to a possibility, misconceived as it may be in actuality, they are themselves one of the accidents (the existence of which they deny) that prompt to the search for different procedures, productive and other, i.e., help to encourage the speculation about their possible nature that is one of the circumstances that may predispose to the receptivity required for the intrusion of spontaneous creation.

It may be remarked, to anticipate ill-considered objection, that these critical considerations do not apply to the theoretical analysis of production as such made here, which has nothing whatever to do with any supposed necessity or fact as these are alleged actually to exist in presentiments of failure. The argument that production of its very nature is accompanied by unknowable residues (first Nature) is of no practical significance whatever, and could not be without self-contradiction. Within the very terms of the argument, the association of the idea of unknowable residues (first Nature) with some presentiment of doom is absurd, requiring the unknowable to be known as at least so associated. The idea of first Nature is of value only theoretically, in conjunction with the related idea of second Nature and homo faber nature, ideas of a like wholly abstract character useful mainly in connection with the re-examination of the idea of freedom, of radical social change and what these betoken. The aim of the reconsideration of the nature of production as such is purely critical: to show, *inter alia*, that the mere restriction of production in the narrow sense (what was suggested as "zero growth") would resolve none of the present problems definitively (assuming that in conditions of general competition zero growth would be at all possible the world overall, even under a tyranny extending to the entire globe); and to show at the same time that the practical suggestions that can alone be made today, revolutionary as they may appear, are inescapably of a kind that must yield such a result, given the limits set by society as exhaustive hypothesis informing second Nature and homo faber nature to the possibility of perception, knowledge, and experience, that is to say, one necessarily confined to what actually is so.

It may seem platitudinous to remark that all such practical suggestions refer, and can only refer, to present problems. The consequences of this are, however, not often well understood. "Conservation", for example, seems a self-evidently reasonable, practical (and practicable) suggestion in the light of the ravages made by present production. Yet the moment it be asked in terms of what the determination of that to be conserved, and of the extent and manner of its conservation, is to be made, if it is to be rational, difficulties arise. For in order to be so rational, its necessity with respect to the struggle for survival requires to be exhibited. Relative to the given struggle, for the survival of the existing, produced second Nature and homo faber nature that are its terms, this is not possible, since what is necessary to it (so far as available knowledge and experience enable such a determination to be made, whether real or illusory, something foreknowlege is not permitted us) is what is actually taking place, which is just what has given rise to the idea of conservation as an imperative need. The necessity involved by conservation must thus have a quite other ground, in brief, the belief that the given struggle for existence threatens to make survival as such impossible. That is to say, its ground must be the struggle for survival as such, and the resources and productive processes imputed to it. About this, however, no knowledge is possible, no experience. It follows that any determination about what is to be conserved made in terms of it can but be the outcome of some dogmatic presupposition concerning what the struggle for survival as such is fancied to need. So far as concerns the actual struggle for survival, of which alone there can be knowledge and experience (knowledge and experience that are themselves produced by it as effect and cause), it is the very possibility (real or not) of the exhaustion of some resources that, *inter alia*, impels to the attempt to find others to replace them, a replacement that always involves associated changes in production techniques, in capacities simultaneously with material. Since every such replacement alters second Nature and homo faber nature within the range of its application in unforeseeable fashion, opening up possibilities and connected effects wholly beyond present ken, possibilities and effects that could not have been foreknown to lie within the range of second Nature and homo faber nature, that is, to be means for carrying on the struggle for survival in a basically unaltered way, it is impossible, from a rational standpoint, to assert that this struggle is in process of becoming self-defeating (as the alleged "ecological crisis," for example), however much it may appear to do so, from the vantage point of present production and its effects upon presently known resources, upon second Nature and homo faber nature as now constituted. The conservation, or rather, to mark the difference, the husbanding of resources is therefore necessary and rational only in connection with present production, with the continuance of the struggle for survival in its present form, since there can be no foreknowledge of what may constitute the resources of a future production, a future struggle, even though basically unchanged. It may then happen that the very resources needing now to be husbanded cease to be so in coming to be no longer needed, which has precisely that effect. The apparently platitudinous remark has the unplatitudinous consequence that the conception of future problems (such as is involved by the presuppositions of conservation, as well, be it said at once, as by those at work in other fields) is necessarily a misconception, that the solutions to these proposed, practical as they may appear in such terms, are, from the standpoint of the present that is all that can be rationally available to us, always impracticable in general, and the more so, the more radical they seem to be. This notwithstanding, they still can have features that can be of present use; and to the extent that they have, and that these are exploited, they achieve the reverse of what was intended, enlarging the means of the given, conventional struggle for survival, and contributing to the continuance of what they aimed to prevent.

Conservation, presented as a radical alternative to existing society, has an inherent tendency to be both regressive and self-contradictory, since, on the one hand, the refusal of existing production processes in any sphere throws it back to earlier ones (so far as there can be knowledge of them), and, on the other, the "alternative technology" proposed, in the form in which it could alone, relative to existing second Nature and homo faber nature, conceivably really constitute such an alternative, is both an outgrowth of existing technology and dependent upon it. "Back to Nature" associated especially with the regress, to an alleged more simple life, a life invariably conceived as being "organically" more in harmony with "Nature" and so *eo ipso* more satisfying, is a fantasy resting upon a misunderstanding of what production as such necessarily involves that derives ultimately from acceptance of the reflection theory of consciousness.

All production, the very constitution of second Nature and homo faber nature, bespeaks the creative reconstitution of what was originally, that, in the very act of becoming alone knowable and known to us as so reconstituted, becomes unknowable as what it was originally and as what remains of it in the form of residues (first Nature). From the standpoint of the unknown original, production necessarily bespeaks interference, a circumstance that gives point to Kierkegaard's view of knowledge as an indiscretion relative to "Nature". The ravage of "Nature" such interference involves is, to confine myself to this here, the *conditio sine qua non* of the human struggle for survival, the mode of which is production. It is *a fortiori* then the condition of the creation, production, and re-production of the possibilities which could other than as a result of such "ravage" not become actual as objective, objectified capacities, and properties of material and agent. This "ravage" in any of its manifold forms, as also in general, may have a critical point beyond which the damage inflicted no longer can have a productive function, at least in terms of available knowledge and experience. But (the dialectical "law" of the change of quantity into quality notwithstanding), to constitute such a critical point as knowledge, to determine in advance of its having been reached, precisely when and how it will do so, and thus to anticipate and prevent it, is in the nature of knowledge impossible. Prospectively, its existence can never be other than a supposition, the legitimacy of which cannot be rationally established, however much evidence there may appear to be in support of it. The very supposition, should it result in what are considered to be needed countermeasures, such as a ban on certain forms of production, or a restriction of production as a whole (assuming this to be a practicable possibility, which is doubtful), constitutes a bar to knowledge, the measures themselves, if they have the success desired, making it impossible ever to determine whether they were actually necessary or not. For, here again, the ground for action is present knowledge and experience, present problems, present possibilities, in terms of which the future is unavoidably predicted, and comes to be, in this necessarily incorrect predetermination, a factor determining judgment of what has to be done. In the nature of production in general as the constitution of society as unknowable exhaustive hypothesis informing perception, knowledge, and experience, and absolutely limiting them to the thereby given second Nature and homo faber nature, there never can be any independent reality (let alone actuality) that can serve as a ground for judging the viability of existing society. The supposition underlying the idea of being in harmony with "Nature", that is part of the doctrine of conservation, is without foundation, in that, *inter alia*, it stipulates a determinable, i.e., determinate relation between two terms, one of which is absolutely unknowable in virtue of the very fact that the other has been constituted as knowable—a relation thus *a priori* unknowable in the very nature of production. By the same token the idea of disharmony with "Nature" is as unknowable a relation.

Harmony as a determinable, determinate relation is a production category, as is disharmony, both being wholly confined to second Nature. What falls within the limits of finite teleology is *ipso facto* harmonious, i.e., the several production processes in question, the capacities and properties of material and agent involved, have been so determined, so produced, as to work smoothly together to the purposed end, and unavoidable accident apart, are thus in harmony. What is for any reason not so amenable to finite teleological determination, to being produced, manifests a want of harmony. The disharmony of society as a whole relates not to "Nature", as conservation supposes, but to its own second Nature, strictly, to itself, witness to the fact that it itself as this second Nature has not as a whole become subject to finite teleological determination, production. The idea, basic to conservation, that a return to earlier production bespeaks the restoration of a harmony (balance, equilibrium, however it may be called) is an illusion. The reality, were it possible, would be a return not to "Nature" but to a previously existing second Nature, to, for the generality of men, a mode of toilsome existence with meagre and uncertain rewards, no longer common today precisely there, where conservation in this regressive form is being advocated—something wholly unimaginable as a result of unconstrained choice, given the present nature of homo faber, its needs, and expectations. That is to say, all such a return could re-establish would be a different kind of disharmony that, that previous society taken as a whole, led to its collapse, once having become general and irremediable in the then given terms.

The condition of harmony has heretofore never obtained, other than perhaps (so far as can be judged despite the lack of all possible actual experience) as exceptionally and precariously in some small earlier society "primitive" to us. At most there have otherwise at times, and in some few societies, been more or less long periods of relative stability, the result always of oppression, and characterised, for the mass of people, by suffering and want, conditions ill-suited to the harmony conservation imagines itself to be restoring. If it is to be at all, harmony can only be a condition of existence beyond the social limitations of present second Nature and homo faber nature, about which clearly nothing fruitful can be said.

The significance of the regressive tendency of conservation becomes clear in this connection, and shows itself to advantage in so-called "intermediate technology." The usefulness of labour-intensive production processes to relieve crass poverty wherever existing technology can in present circumstances only worsen social conditions is, of course, not in question. What is, is the putting forward of such processes as an alternative to existing technology as such, on the supposition that the social problems resulting from this technology are irresolvable. Indeed, from the standpoint both of second Nature, i.e., of the unrestrained and determining struggle for survival the outcome of which is, for the generality, dependent upon labour, upon employment, all social palliatives notwithstanding, as of homo faber nature, the organising principle of which is social productive labour, it is difficult to conceive of a solution with present means and knowledge. But the concept of such a standpoint itself points to there being in principle possibilities beyond it. Failing this, however, "intermediate technology" may well seem attractive as a practical way out of what presently seems an impasse out of which there is no way but that of retreat. Yet its effect would be to reaffirm and perhaps intensify the very servitude (and inescapably accompanying tyranny) existing technology, the development of which it would have the effect of arresting, alone can in principle help to bring to an end as a fundamental condition of human existence. For it is this technology, for all its evident dangers and accompanying problems, that, by taking over from homo faber capacities and properties that heretofore necessarily made man an essential instrument, or agent, or production, for the first time makes this no longer so. Production itself, that is, by making direct human labour no longer its basic condition, allows the possibility of life beyond the confines of the struggle for survival (at least in respect of a portion of it presently indeterminable) to be envisaged as capable at least in principle of being made actual. That this is a quite fanciful (if perhaps logical) deduction, is something that may not be legitimately asserted, i.e., predetermined. That it may never become actual is another matter. Both are here irrelevant. What is relevant is only that the possibility, however abstractly in given conditions, can properly be envisaged as a consequence of modern technology, and of it alone. For from this it follows that, were it ever to be given effect in actuality, it could be only by, *inter alia*, coming to terms with technology such as it had come to be at the time in question, in the light of the requirements disclosed by perception, knowledge, and experience of the demands and needs of the radically new purpose involved. It might well be that such perception, knowledge, and experience would show some forms of technology to be (as Ellul, for one, asserts) *sui generis* incompatible with these requirements, and others to be so only to a limited extent, matters clearly not capable of being discussed, let alone decided, in advance. It might even be that, owing to such a decision, a full or partial return to earlier more laborious production processes in one or another sphere of production came to be seen to be unavoidable. This, however, would be a far different matter from the return presently advocated by conservation, in that its ground would still be the needs of existence beyond the confines of the struggle for survival, for the sake of which such a return would have been decided upon. Whereas with respect to conservation, lacking any conception of such an existence and (even had it one) any possibility in given conditions of putting it into practice, the return represents nothing but an intensification of the struggle for survival from which, with the removal of modern technology in great part, the very possibility of life beyond this struggle vanishes.

Nothing said requires as a consequence that all forms of technology must today be simply accepted. What does follow is that all decisions relating to technology with respect to its acceptability can but be controversial, in that it is impossible to find any *a priori* unexceptionable grounds for judging present production in terms of the totality of its future effects, its intrinsic accidentality (internal and external) removing all possibility of certainty from their determination. Virtually without exception, judgments that involve the future are inherently not merely of questionable validity, but of one to which it is impossible from the standpoint of the present to give actual determinate, objective, and objectified form and content, the future being, in the given conditions of the struggle for survival, unknowable to us in its actuality, and any necessary predetermination of it demanded by such judgment unavoidably but semblance. Other than perhaps in wholly exceptional instances in which present production appears in some respect definitively to determine the future, radioactive substances being a possible example—and even this falls into the category of the questionable, being based naturally upon present knowledge and the possibilities it alone allows of, knowledge which the future may reveal to have been defective in its limitations to just these possibilities—there can never be an objective, rational ground for any decisions to which such judgments give rise, or can do. Couched as they may be in the form of reason, these decisions in effect reduce themselves to no more than what seems best at the given time in accordance with criteria that, deriving as they do from a wholly suppositious future in terms of which alone they can be established, are without foundation, rationally considered. Production that presently appears, and in some respects may well be, an unqualified danger may nonetheless, accidentally, result in the creation, production, and reproduction of something beneficial that retrospectively may come to be seen to have been a necessary condition for the establishment of a radically new mode of existence beyond (at least in part) the struggle for survival; whereas production presently believed to be beneficial may, just as accidentally, reveal itself to have had dangerous potentialities undreamt of, that made a radically new mode of existence impossible of achievement. This notwithstanding, decisions have to be, and are made; but these, which are practical suggestions carried into effect, always relate exclusively to the present, however much they may be presented as necessary to safeguard the future in some fashion, since, be it that their relatively immediate effects can be correctly determined (and even this is seldom, if ever, possible, given the context of general competition), their more remote ones cannot be. Reason, wholly confined as it is to finite teleology, to that the causality of which has been so determined in accordance with its purposed production as to bring it under the control requisite thereto, compels to the bleak conclusion that irremediable blindness is the inescapable condition of social existence, so long, at least, as it remains basally determined in unknowable manner by the competitive struggle for survival that completely escapes control in its general aspects.

In sum, simple and commonsensical as conservation and associated ideas may appear to be, peremptory as their being put into practice may seem, they nonetheless, in the form of comprehensive generalisations about society and "Nature" (including "human nature") and suggested supposedly radical reorganisation needed to bring the former into "self-sustaining balance" with the latter, derive from premises which, necessarily going beyond what can be rationally established, fall into the realm of semblance, and yield dogmatic, not (for all that they may seem so) rational, prescriptions. These ideas, like others current, are witness to unease about present society, legitimate or not (something to determine which prospectively no means exist, or can exist). Yet, in advance of a radically new hypothesis that alone could provide the means for its correct objective expression and enable measures flowing from this to be cast in the needed teleological terms, something constituted by the very radically new hypothesis itself, such unease, however expressed, be it as conservation or something else, is compelled to use the only means available, those the existing hypothesis about society and Nature that sets the absolute limit to the possibility of perception, knowledge, and experience, alone allows of, albeit that this is the very one from which the unease springs and to which it relates. Its expression in practical terms is thus inescapably entangled in the dilemma of having to call on the devil to drive out Beelzebub. That there is this dilemma is not apparent, nor can it be, failing the idea of the limit just mentioned and a grasp of the wholly reflexive mechanism of perception and cognition, a want that is a prime cause of the inability to distinguish knowledge (or rationality) from semblance. Not that the perception that this dilemma exists, and an analysis of what it consists in (so far as this can be done), can resolve it, the hypothetical nature of society (and of the Nature and human nature produced by it accordant with it), in which it inheres, being of its nature beyond the perception, knowledge, and experience available, so long as it remains their informing presupposition. The dilemma, that is, can be no more than a purely abstract idea in existing conditions. What alone is possible, in relation to it, is to show the presumption of there being presently possible perception, knowledge, and experience beyond their, for us, actual absolute (social) limits, to be, so long as these hold, an illusion productive only of confusion and error.

These are seen to advantage in an idea associated with conservation (though not exclusively with it), that organisms other than man also have, "by Nature," a "right" to existence, viz., that this "right" is, as a right, "natural", in a sense that its perception is no more than the reflection of something "in Nature" that exists as such independently of the human struggle for survival.

For the struggle for survival in itself, be it human or other, no such right, however, exists. The seemingly indiscriminate destructiveness of the human struggle for survival compared with that of other organisms is an appearance merely. The supposition that there is here a real distinction, that entails a difference in kind between the human and all other forms of the struggle for survival, is a fallacy. Every particular struggle for survival has a form and extent consonant with the specific need (or needs) the satisfaction of which bespeaks its successful prosecution. In itself, i.e., within the limits set by such need (or needs), the struggle is without limit, once the satisfaction of need (or needs) comes into question, or, as earlier put, the competition intrinsic to it is, within the set limits, at full pitch. So far as it takes place at all, its destructiveness is indiscriminate with respect to that the destruction of which is the condition of its successful issue. The qualification, in effect, loses all point with the vanishing of the distinction it was supposed to mark. The error (basal to any idea of some "natural right to existence") springs from the failure to distinguish between the struggle for survival as such (what it necessarily involves) and the several appearances its specific expressions of more, or less, limited needs, take on, when seen from the standpoint of the human struggle for survival, if this be uncritically taken to be fundamentally different from all others. This failure itself once more stems from the reflection theory of consciousness.

To achieve a perspective free of anthropocentrism is impossible, given that the "nature" alone knowable to men, second Nature, is that which men have themselves produced, is the result of their struggle for survival and unalterably stamped with the egocentricity basal to that struggle. The belief that man alone is capable of production is groundless, the struggle for survival being as such but the struggle for self-production and repro-duction that always and necessarily includes the productive transforma-tion of the environment to the extent needed by the requirements of that struggle. The view that organisms, other than man, are essentially passive, are, so to say, biologically "programmed", such that will and purpose can hardly be ascribed to them, derives from their status in human second

Nature and reflects their necessary function of means purely in the human production and reproduction in which man's struggle for survival consists. That is to say, what those organisms are for us, what we constitute their nature to be in accordance with our needs and purposes is one thing; what they are in and to themselves, what their nature is outside human second Nature, a different one, one of which no perception, knowledge, and experience is possible to us, a difference arising from the nature of production itself, as earlier shown.

The supposition flowing from the reflection theory of consciousness, that what is "Nature" for man is "Nature" to all other organisms, differences and limitations granted, thus becomes untenable. The assumption underlying this, that "Nature" independently of man is essentially as it results from man's production of it, and capable of being represented "in itself" as a development to man, such that the *scala natura* articulating this development can be taken to be actual—the only possible ground for believing that all organic forms within their limits share the same "Nature" that comes to fullness only with (and in) man—this assumption necessary to natural history exhibits the inescapable error of all historical representation, the transformation of something looked upon as the end (here man) into a supposedly actual, and actually determining, immanent teleological necessity, shaping a development having this result. Natural history, the theory of evolution (however conceived), cannot help but have recourse to the dialectic of potentiality and actuality, it being the representation of "Nature" in the only fashion in which it can become amenable to conception, as a process of production. As such, taken as a whole, it is beyond all possibility of being scientifically established, there being no means whereby it could in the needed comprehensive manner ever be translated into the actuality requisite thereto. It is, like all other history, semblance, albeit, like some history, unavoidable, if any appearance of rationality is to be given to what but for this would remain sheer unintelligible fortuity. Natural history as a whole, that is, is one of the necessary and necessarily ordered appearances in terms of which the unknown original (whatever it may be in itself) can alone come to be produced as the semblance of knowledge, viz., it is the articulation of "Nature" as if it had been produced by man, his second Nature, and has, considered in its particularities, actuality, is scientific and rational, to the extent that any aspects of it are capable of, and become, the objective and objectified results of production, and that extent alone. What becomes actual is thus not, on that account, to be taken to be (to that extent) the "truth" of "Nature in itself." It is self-evident that the categories "truth" and "falsity" cannot have reference to the unknown. That they can alone have reference to the known means, however, that their field of application is wholly restricted to that which has been produced as such. But, as earlier argued, the very act of production constituting an object as knowable in accordance with some specific purpose (and no object is otherwise capable of being constituted or of becoming knowable), simultaneously makes the residue of that out of which it has been formed unknowable, this being the condition of there being any determination to objectivity at all. Taken as a whole, then, second Nature in whatever form produced, and to whatever extent, i.e., any possible remaining unknown being wholly irrelevant to the matter at hand, becomes knowable only on the condition of its being itself the absolute bar to our ever being able to know what "Nature" may be aside from second Nature. Second Nature itself, that is, establishes "Nature" as other than itself as *a priori* unknowable. It is thus impossible (and pointless) to attribute truth (or falsity) to second Nature as a whole with respect to "Nature in itself," there being for us no possible external point of reference in terms of which this might become capable of being determined. A second Nature can, to itself, constitute, and indeed has historically constituted, such a point of reference retrospectively, with respect to another second Nature it has displaced; but no more on this account yields knowledge of "Nature in itself" than did that one. The assertion of defect or inadequacy in existing second Nature in terms of some supposed relation to "Nature in itself" is thus *a priori* without any possibility of scientific foundation, and of its nature incapable of translation into corrective practical and practicable measures answering to the intended purpose (except, perhaps, by sheerest chance, which of course does not alter the matter).

If "Nature in itself" is inaccessible to man in virtue of what necessarily occurs in the human struggle for survival, for self-production and reproduction, a fundamental contradiction would arise, were it not to be assumed that this is so also for all other organisms engaged, in their several ways, in a like struggle, viz., that every one of these organisms produces a second Nature peculiar to itself in accordance with its self-productive and reproductive needs, and, like man, perceives, knows, and experiences "Nature," in whatever fashion it may do so, in the terms and limits set by these alone. There are, then, as many second Natures as there are varieties of organisms. To the extent, moreover, slight as it may be, that there are differences in the constitution of organisms of the same kind as individuals, to that extent will their specific second Natures differ in the subordinate features corresponding to these. But for these internal and associated external differences (if any of the latter there be), it would be impossible to account for the variations in the manifested capacity of organisms of the same kind to adapt to environmental changes; or rather, to avoid the realist "Nature in itself" implications of so formulated an idea of adaptation, to determine these, and that capacity jointly, in some fashion, as for and to themselves objective and objectified actualities, as effects of a productive process carried out by themselves that establishes the new relation in question, and simultaneously constitutes second Nature and the nature of the organism concerned, to that extent, afresh.

Insofar as any organism appears and functions as a means to the satisfaction of the needs of another, it does so in this capacity purely, viz., it exists in this relation solely as a constituent of the second Nature of the organism the need of which it satisfies, its nature there being exhausted in this, its function, such that what it may be to itself as other than this, and the second Nature therewith accordant, become, in this context, wholly irrelevant, a matter of absolute indifference. Such indifference to what means may be as other than means is, as earlier argued, a *sine qua non* of production as such and, so, an inherent character of the struggle for survival considered as a process of self-production and reproduction. This indifference extends to what, for any second Nature, does not, and cannot, function as means; that is to say, the criterion for inclusion in second Nature is need in its comprehensive sweep and definition, in terms of which alone is the determination of means as object, as a thus and in no other way constituted objective and objectified actuality, possible. What is beyond the scope of any second Nature established by need, produced in terms of it, not merely has no, but cannot have any, actual objective, objectified existence for the organism whose second Nature this is; and if it manifest itself, must do so as a disturbance, in the degree of its severity, destructive of the "natural order of things," a disturbance the course and nature of which are *sui generis* unknowable to the organism in actuality, whatever fanciful representations of this it may give it in terms of the perception, knowledge, and experience alone available to it and necessarily inapposite to the purpose.

The egocentricity characteristic of the human struggle for survival is no perversity peculiar to it. It inheres in production as such as a finite teleological process, one wholly determined by the purposed result that sets aside as an obstacle to its realisation all that does not function as the means accordant with that end, viz., necessarily denies this actuality within this context. All struggles for survival, in that they are struggles for self-production and reproduction, are thus necessarily egocentric. Were it possible for organisms other than man to represent "Nature" to themselves as a development in the way man does, each of them would, like him, unavoidably conceive itself to be its culmination, to be that by whose ultimate existence the entire process had been from the first determined and directed. Survival, to any organism, cannot but appear as the single end to effect which "Nature" is "in itself" constituted, there being, for any organism, no possible representation of "Nature in itself" other than in terms of the perception, knowledge, and experience alone available to it, those lying within the absolute limits set by the second Nature (and its own) produced by it which in actuality does have the survival of the organism whose second Nature and nature these are as the one end to which it is devoted. I recall here the remark of Wendt to the effect that to any other animal man is but a side-branch of evolution. That is to say, if human second Nature is inescapably anthropocentric owing to its being determined by, and established as, that which meets the needs of the human struggle for survival, so, *mutatis mutandis*, is the second Nature of every other organism likewise inescapably and unalterably constituted in its own image. This being so, it follows that every second Nature, *qua* itself, constitutes a world wholly and irrefragably independent of all others, the perception, knowledge, and experience of which is accordingly impossible to any but the organism whose second Nature any second Nature is. The "thing in itself" (whatever it may be—in general "Nature in itself") is as unperceivable, unknowable, and incapable of being experienced by any organism, as it is by man. All that any organism, man included, can perceive, know, and experience is what it itself has determined and established, viz., produced as the only possible objective and objectified actuality to it, of its nature incommunicable to any other not of its kind, or even of its own kind, to the extent that, as a particular species, or member of it, in some respects differently constituted, it so far has a different second Nature and accordant perception, knowledge, and experience in some respect peculiar to itself.

Every organism, then, carries on its struggle for survival, its self-productive and reproductive activities, in a world of its own, to which all others, insofar as no part of them forms a constituent of its own second Nature, are absolutely irrelevant. These others, if they appear at all, which they may well do at times, can do so only as the intrusion of something inconceivable, and incomprehensible, whatever may be its effects, whether for good or ill. If there were what might properly be called "the balance of Nature," i.e., of "Nature in itself," it could never become an objective and objectified actuality accessible to any organism (man included), since, for it to come about, all second Natures, the interrelations of which were so constituted as to yield this result, would have to figure as subordinate elements in a whole that comprehend them all and was, as necessarily different from any of them, *eo ipso* beyond the absolute limits set by every one of them to the perception, knowledge, and experience possible to it. So far as it can be rationally considered, this to us intrinsically hypothetical "balance of Nature" cannot, if it at all does so, be said to arise by necessity. To suppose this would be to suppose it teleologically determined as part of the production of "Nature in itself" as a whole, a supposition which, however the power capable of producing it be conceived, is self-contradictory; for, unless it be assumed that there be some production, some finite teleological activity of a nature other than that of which we alone have knowledge and so inconceivable to us (an assumption for which there can be no possible rational ground), this production, this finite teleology, can yield but another second Nature to which "Nature in itself" must once more be unknowable and inaccessible, and so on in infinite regress. Short of this, there remains only the conclusion that, assuming there to be one, the "balance of Nature" comes, and can come, about only accidentally, as a result of the in their very nature wholly unintended effects the manifold struggles for survival yield, both in themselves and in consequence of their being carried on simultaneously, isolated as they may be from one another so far as the several organisms involved are concerned, some of which effects (in the case of man at least) may in principle be knowable, and others *a priori* unknowable, being presumed to be associated with the first Nature the constitution of a second Nature brings about.

The idea of the "balance of Nature" thus has, and can have, no relation to "Nature in itself," and conceived as having so falls, like it, into the realm semblance. The idea, however, becomes altogether different, so far as man is concerned (to limit myself to him) if it be viewed as the expression of a need of second Nature, one that has come to the fore owing to the disturbance resulting from modern production, viz., to that which is often expressed as a want of balance that seems to threaten the very possibility of survival itself, to destroy second Nature as we know and experience it. This balance, that relates wholly to second Nature, i.e., has reference to its production, to the needs that impel thereto, is, at least in principle, capable of becoming perceived, known, and experienced, of being given the objective, objectified actuality as a determinate teleological process determined to that end, to being produced and established, even though only within the absolute limits set by the nature of production itself as such, as accompanied always by unknowable residues (first Nature), the effects of which, though they may be felt in some way, are themselves equally unknowable both as being associated with first Nature, and for what they actually are. But the achievement of this argues a radically different hypothesis about society, man, and Nature, since what has led to that which appears to be a lack of balance self-evidently results from the hypothesis now ruling which, in its appearance of expressing the true nature of society, man, and Nature, prevents any present possibility of our discovering what such a balance might require *in concreto*, the conditions needful to the purpose, among which are plainly a basally altered perception of the nature of society, man, and Nature.

The struggle for survival, for all that it may fitly and usefully be considered in itself, never takes place in actuality as other than a struggle to satisfy the specific needs of some organism whose struggle it is (to determine, constitute, and establish the means, which always includes the capacities required to that end)—which needs thus determine its particular form and content.

So far as appertains to this struggle, need of whatever kind manifests itself as a peremptory demand for satisfaction, is inherently aggressive and, relative to what is required for this satisfaction, competitive, in that, as to it means simply to that end, it sets itself against whatever else that which is to be constituted means may be in and to itself, the struggle for satisfaction being *eo ipso* a struggle to deny to this whatever would prevent its becoming such means. Every need thus of its very nature constitutes and establishes aggression and competition as fundamental

relations, relations which, as earlier shown, are necessarily just as fundamental to production, which is but the translation of need into the activity
leading to its satisfaction. The question raised by Adorno, in the light of
what seemed to him to be an essential condition for a radically new,
peaceable society, whether aggression could properly be regarded as a
contingent, not a necessary, factor in human existence, and so, in principle, capable of being excluded from social relations, thus shows itself
to be based on a false premise.

Satisfaction achieved, the need (at least temporarily) vanishes, and
with it the relations it set in train. Supposing there were an organism
whose struggle for survival involved only one single need, one whose
second Nature, thus world, was limited to itself *qua* pertinent capacity
and to that which met this need. The appeasement of this need for so
long as it was so, would leave it, so far as it itself was concerned (i.e., for
so long as it itself was not constituted means to the satisfaction of the need
of another organism, a relation established not by, but against, it, independently of itself), out of relation to that which constituted its world, indifferent to it. It would, thus, be indifferent both to that which in the context
of need figured as means but now could (and presumably would), as
other than this, exist in unchallenged independence, and to itself as the
capacity established exclusively in connection with, and so in terms of,
this need upon the satisfaction of which its survival was wholly and
uniquely dependent. So wanting this (in this hypothetical context) only
relation in terms of which, as the need demanding satisfaction by something other than itself, it could become conscious of the world external to
itself constituted thereby, it would simultaneously want the retroactive
effect of that relation whereby alone its wholly reflexively established self-
consciousness could come about, even in so stringently limited a manner
and substance as would follow from its having constituted itself as nothing
but the capacity demanded by that single need. For so long as the need
was not re-awakened, for so long, that is, as its struggle for survival was
intermitted by the satisfaction of the single need therein involved, for so
long would the organism, now altogether beyond the imperative urging
of the necessity determining, or ruling, its existence when in quest of
survival, be in a state that, relative to its second Nature incarnation, to the
perception, knowledge, and experience alone available to it (entirely
second Nature determinations), must appear one of wholly quiescent
un(self)consciousness, of nothingness. In this state which, whatever it
may be, is nothingness only from the standpoint of second Nature, witness
to the impossibility of our ever being able to perceive, know, and experience in what it consists, the organism would be, in accord with Kant's
view of freedom as that which lies beyond all possible rule, free.

The foregoing assumption is doubtless altogether abstract, of interest
only as a hypothetical simplification elucidating, *inter alia*, the circumstances in which freedom in this its strictly correct definition can, if at all,

be properly envisaged as arising. That the difficulties attendant upon this in practice should appear insuperable is not astonishing, given the human nature alone conceivable to us, that constituted in terms of, and determined by, the struggle for survival. More pertinent here, however, is the theoretical consequence that, since freedom is wholly beyond conception as what it may be, the perception, knowledge, and experience alone available to us necessarily making it appear as a condition of utter want of anything determinable, discussion of these circumstances from its standpoint is impossible without self-contradiction. For the attempt to do so requires that it be considered as an end to which, and in terms of which, human society is in accordant finite teleological fashion to be radically reconstituted and re-established, something *a priori* impossible, if knowledge of what freedom is and involves be, as it is, absolutely denied us. To point the self-contradiction: If this knowledge were available to us, if, that is, freedom were transformed into a need demanding satisfaction, it would at once be brought within the orbit of rule-guided determination, and become thereby but the imposition in some form of the servitude intrinsic to production. It follows that what can be discussed belongs entirely to the struggle for survival, has no, and cannot have any, determinable connection with freedom, the association of which with necessity in any way at all, be it the most indirect and tenuous, can result only in absurdity, something further consideration of which is neither pertinent nor interesting.

From the simplification it becomes apparent that with the satisfaction of need, the indifference that before related only to what the means thereto might be as other than means, becomes absolute. What is supposed the "right to existence" is in reality this manifestation of utter indifference of satisfied need to that which, insofar as need compels to recognition of it as existing, exists, and can exist, only in the determined and determinate form and substance of means, and as so and so only, given objective and objectified actuality. In the context of the struggle for survival, the acknowledgment of something as existing is *ipso facto* the assertion of its being purely means to the satisfaction of need, or, what is the same, the denial of its "right to existence" as other than this. Only that which, temporarily or permanently, has not been so determined to existence, has the possibility of independent life, a condition that comes about by accident as a result of circumstances wholly beyond the possibility of being produced by any organism (other than perhaps quite exceptionally), supervening as it does upon the cessation of production; and not at all, as is implied by the idea of "right", by necessity, in virtue simply of an organism's being in being. The bare schematic presentation is admittedly subject to qualification *in concreto*, and is to that extent not a completely adequate representation of the behaviour exhibited by organisms amidst the manifold varieties of the circumstances and vicissitudes in which they lead their lives. Yet, susceptible of alteration as they may be, even to the extent of seemingly being set aside in exceptional conditions, the intrinsic requirements of the struggle for survival can never be done away with, expressing as they do the absolutely limiting conditions necessary for its prosecution.

This notwithstanding, the assumption of a "right to existence" is not to be dismissed as mere sentimental nonsense. Some such ground for criticism of modern society is unavoidable, so long as the nature of the struggle for survival as such, of self-production and reproduction, i.e., of production as such, has not been thoroughly examined. Failing this, the in the given circumstances necessarily misconceived, differences between the human struggle for survival and those of other organisms appear explainable only on the supposition of their constituting a difference in kind, such that, if the latter be taken (as they commonly are) to be in accord with "Nature", the former needs must come to be considered in some sense "unnatural".

To superficial view, the purely accidental result of the relatively limited needs of the struggles for survival of organisms other than man, namely, the persistence of the several organisms in mutual independence (other things being equal), readily suggests some necessity at work, some "natural law" directing and controlling the behaviour of these organisms and determining their relations among themselves to that end, one which properly seems definable as the "right to existence." This taken to be so, there easily results an idea of "Nature" as a lawful, grand design in which all (man alone excepted) play their allotted parts, one in which competition appears "naturally" subordinated to cooperation, the imputed behaviour accordant therewith coming, in consequence, plausibly to be taken as evidence of a "natural morality," one in terms of which man and his struggle for survival as asserted exception are then judged and necessarily found wanting. The anthropocentric nature of this conception is plain. As we have no perception, knowledge, and experience whatever other than that which arises in terms of human production, viz., no possible way of conceiving of anything as necessarily coming to be what it is, except as the outcome of a process of production such as we carry on ourselves (for to conceive of it as having come about accidentally is but to acknowledge that we in actuality have, or can have, no conception of how it did so), it ensues that "Nature", if it is to be represented as such a lawful, grand design, must be assumed to have been produced by someone in accordance with this as end; must, that is, and can, be conceived only in the terms requisite thereto alone available to us, those proper only to the finite teleological procedure of production. Absolutely nothing available to perception, knowledge, and experience can possibly warrant such a representation as rational which, for all its once undoubted usefulness as semblance, now constitutes but an obstacle to understanding. Even were this not so, nothing would be substantially altered, in that the resulting representation would merely be, as in the circumstance earlier examined, the first step in an infinite regress, to prevent which some dogmatic postulate would have be resorted to, another unmoved mover of the universe, Absolute Idea, matter as intrinsically creative, or whatever it may be. Such shifts set aside, and nothing invoked but what the perception, knowledge, and experience we have, make available conclusively or inferentially, what has been said becomes the only possible rational representation of the matter in general (granted the need for alteration in detail). This, of course, does not tell us what happens in "Nature" ("in itself"), absolutely unknowable to us. What it does tell us is that, unless there be a kind of production, a kind of struggle for survival, the nature of which is basally different from our own and so inconceivable to us (a supposition from the standpoint of reason as wholly arbitrary as it is needless), every productive act, every struggle for survival, of any organism whatsoever, simply in virtue of being so, inherently has, and must have, these and these features, must constitute these and these relations as fundamental, and yield these and these effects, no matter that their manifestation *in concreto* be endlessly varied, owing to the accidentality of the circumstances inescapably set in train by these very productive acts, these very struggles for survival, themselves, both singly and inter-relatedly. This being so, namely, it being established that, rationally considered, no basal difference can be supposed between the human and all other struggles for survival, *qua* self-productive and reproductive activities, the differences among them become explicable in like rational fashion.

These differences, so far as they are amenable to rational understanding, resolve themselves into one, the scope of the second Natures determined and established by the needs of the several struggles for survival, i.e., by what these constrain the organisms in question to produce as their only possible specific second Natures and natures *qua* these organisms (which always come about simultaneously). From the standpoint alone available to us, what lies beyond human second Nature is exhausted in its representation as a manifold of interconnected, but nonetheless wholly independent, second Natures of, relative to the various organisms, a more or less limited scope. Beyond the confines of every one of these lies that (whatever it may be) to which they are all severally absolutely indifferent, as to something which to them, in terms of their only available perception, knowledge, and experience (be the natures of these what they may severally be), does not, and cannot, exist. The appearance of what is misconceived as *suum cuique* actually existing "in Nature" is thus the effect not only of satisfied need, but also of its limitations.

Anything added to this bare representation involves anthropocentric imputation. Given the already mentioned specific nature of the struggle for survival *in concreto*, even with respect to members of one species so far as these exhibit variations of any import, it becomes impossible to make distinctions in the behaviour of organisms (man included) with respect to what is essential to the struggle for survival and what not, without prejudicial interpretation, viz., without the imposition of criteria alien to the matter. For these criteria must have as their ground some pre-determination of what constitutes the struggle for survival in essence, inevitably a crude abstraction. Their validity is thus *a priori* unestablishable with reference to that to which they supposedly relate, since criteria and ground themselves contain implicitly the interpretation presented as a result seemingly arisen by induction; have pre-established this as the result. In connection with the struggle for survival of organisms other than man "in themselves," unknowable to us in virtue of the absolutely closed nature of human second Nature (as of all others), the results obtained cannot be other than semblance, plausible as they may appear. As expression of human needs, of determinations established as part of the human struggle for survival, of human second Nature and homo faber nature, these can be rational and scientific results. That is to say, the determination of what in the human struggle for survival shall constitute the needs of organisms other than man, of what shall be allowed them, has reference not to them as they may be in themselves (unknowable to us), but to them in virtue of their function of means to the satisfaction of human needs, to the prosecution of the human struggle for survival, as so and in no other way determined and constituted as objective and objectified, as actually existing for man. This, the required qualifications granted, holds also of men themselves, insofar as, relative to production, some have in appearance functioned solely as means, a circumstance that gives point to the remark attributed to Aristotle, that "Nature" erred in giving slaves the form of human beings.

VI

What distinguishes the human struggle for survival from that of all other organisms is the multiplicity and variety of needs therein involved. The second Nature constituted in terms of these is thus likewise more extensive and comprehensive than are the second Natures of other organisms, as are the properties and capacities of material and agent associated therewith. It is this that gives the human struggle for survival its (misconceived) appearance of sheerly indiscriminate destructiveness, the fact that to meet these needs, production has to be accordingly varied and extensive, to leave, so it seems, nothing "in Nature" untouched, be the consequences what they may be, an impression as false as its ground, the reflection theory. In reality, what production "touches" "in Nature" is only that which, as part of the human struggle for survival *in concreto*, has been created and produced and reproduced as both effect and cause of need, and constitutes Nature for man out of the original which, before this took place, was unknown, did not exist for him, and presumably, to some extent, remains (and will always remain) unknown and non-existent, productive innovation not having come to a standstill. That is to say, the human struggle for survival, human production, leaves nothing untouched "in Nature," only because "Nature" for it and to it (with its associated perception, knowledge, experience, and capacities that constitute human "nature" as homo faber), is precisely what has been created and produced in terms of that "touch", namely second Nature and homo faber nature. And the same holds, *mutatis mutandis*, for the production, the struggle for survival, the second Nature and capacities of all other organisms as well, underscoring the falsity of the distinctiveness imputed to the human struggle.

So far as the consequences are concerned, they fall into two wholly distinct classes. The first is that of possible consequences *a priori* unknowable for what they actually are, those belonging to the first Nature production brings about in the very act of constituting second Nature, an inescapable feature of all struggles for survival. The second is that of possible consequences that can in principle be known, viz., can, if required, be dealt with within the confines of second Nature, though, owing to the intrinsic accidentality of production, internal and external, not without yielding their own further consequences (aside from the possible unknowable ones the production of the needed measures brings about, as itself giving rise to first Nature in the act of doing so). To the first class, production, the struggle for survival, be it that of any organism at all, is necessarily indifferent, irrespective of whether production be limited or extensive. So far as the second is concerned, whether there be or not indifference to the consequences is to some extent a matter of opinion, since what the consequences are is itself frequently a debatable matter, as already argued.

Every material need, in that what satisfies it has to be produced, sets in train the quantum of competition (aggression, violence) and accidentality, internal and external, inseparable from that production, *ergo* that satisfaction, with respect both to the unknown original, out of which what becomes constituted as material is abstracted, and to that portion of second Nature and homo faber nature thereby constituted. In that such need involves production, it necessarily also involves the servitude intrinsic to finite teleology. The more varied the needs, the more varied is the production required to meet them, and therewith the more extensive the competition (aggression, violence) and accidentality, and *pari passu*, the servitude of the material and agent (homo faber), given actuality merely as the properties and capacities relevant to the requisite production, and existing in that form and content alone, as mere means for it. These are fundamental aspects both of second Nature and of the homo faber nature produced concurrently with it, as part of it, arising out of the very nature of production, of the struggle for survival, as such.

In this abstract, schematic representation, the phrase "material need" is used for simplicity's sake. It is open to misconception, as implying the existence of another kind of need ("non-material") not of its nature competitive and aggressive. This is not so. In actuality, no material need *per se* is ever to be met (other than perhaps quite exceptionally). Every such need is normally always part of a constellation of needs, some of which are "non-material", the particular form, content, significance of which, singly and severally, their importance relative to one another, is determined by the manifold of accidental historical circumstances *in concreto*, always, however, within the absolute limits imposed by the society in which they manifest themselves, *qua* exhaustive hypothesis that determines and restricts the possibilities available even in principle. It is self-evident that no hard and fast notions with respect to needs is at all possible (as has already been argued). In effect, the distinction of material from non-material need falls away, since in actuality it hardly ever happens that a material need is produced that does not of its nature involve the production of non-material need (which has the self-same character of being intrinsically aggressive and competitive), and vice versa.

94

It is conceivable that in terms of crude human need, that required simply for the survival of man *qua* organism merely, there may never have been a time at which production would not have been sufficient for the purpose, other than exceptionally, and the competition (aggression, violence) and accidentality associated with it minimal, little more than that without which this production could not have taken place. That the reverse is the common occurrence shows the falsity and futility of such abstractions, relative to the future, as to the past. In reality, the very notion of survival is at any time and place wholly inseparable from the given produced nature of homo faber, from its expression as what I have earlier called excess relative to the crude abstraction. The conception of what is proper to man, be it in terms of food, occupation, etc., or in terms of self-respect, honour, etc., always gives expression to that excess *in concreto*, is the expression of the nature of homo faber within a second Nature, as these have been produced and given particular objective, objectified actuality, other than which none is possible at that time and place. Those conditions once destroyed, the nature of homo faber and second Nature radically altered, it becomes impossible to know and experience what these needs were in actuality, which disappear with the nature whose needs these specifically were, as does the second nature that accompanied it. Hence the difficulty in crediting what men have been capable of believing to be the gospel truth, once the grounds for that truth have vanished. This difficulty arises from the misconceived assumption that the "nature" of "man" has always been the same essentially. In reality, however, the eye that looked on a slave and perceived only it, knew and experienced a slave in that objective and objectified actuality and that only, as having a nature and needs accordant with it, and as being so, as having these, "by nature," such that the very idea of a slave's being a man in bondage appeared altogether absurd—that eye has wholly vanished. The perception associated with it, that went with it, is today completely inconceivable, other than as a form of duplicity, as a consciously determined perception relative to some "inhuman" purpose, that is known to be, and experienced as, the commission of a wrong that has in some way to be justified.

To say that for the homo faber nature so constituted, slavery is "natural" (a feature of second Nature) is to say that that homo faber nature is itself in all its manifestations, its notions of self-respect, honour, propriety, justice, as of culture, taste, dress, food, and so on (all of which are needs requiring to be met), the effect of that very competition, aggression, violence, that finds expression, *inter alia*, in the production of slavery (and the needs and capacities determined as constituting the nature of a slave, exceptions granted). That is, the production of the one is inseparable from that of the other. Or, better, such notions are not subjective merely; they exist as objective, objectified, actual features of the social world, and are taken as given "in the nature of things" (as, subjectively, the reflection of actuality, which indeed it is) in just that form and content, such that, within this world that expresses the ruling exhaustive hypothesis about Nature and man for so long as it endures, it is almost wholly impossible to conceive of notions of such a kind as do not imply the necessity of slavery and what goes with it, i.e., of a human nature to which slavery is not an essential requisite. This being so, the excess that these notions, these needs, manifest in being what they are in actuality (and the complementary want that is an aspect of excess on the other side of the scale) can never be perceived to be so from the standpoint for which these are, and can only be, "natural". From this standpoint also, then, the labour and materials required for their satisfaction (something that always involves the pertinent social arrangements safeguarding them), collective and individual, must self-evidently be considered as necessary and well-used, however much they may appear as a thorough misuse and waste of resources from another, radically different, standpoint.

This, *mutatis mutandis*, is so of all homo faber natures, the needs of which, be they the most "spiritual", are, in that they are grounded in the injustice (competition, aggression, violence) intrinsic to their production (in itself, and *in concreto* which determines the forms this will take in actuality), always informed thereby in such fashion as is determined by the particular accidental historical circumstances obtaining at any time. That differences in the behaviour of the same person (as, for example, towards equals and towards slaves) can, to a later different homo faber nature, seem inexplicable other than as a perversity, indicates not that these differences were not in their time and within the then given context wholly normal and appropriate (such that it was the lack of them that appeared a perversity demanding explanation). It indicates that the later nature and its context are so fundamentally different as to make some such assumption inevitable, if explanation, sc. semblance of understanding, be sought for something that in its day would have been taken, and could only have been taken, as self-explanatory, as self-evidently proper and natural.

The fact that such notions as right, justice, honour, propriety, etc., (together with the needs thereto related) are what they are only *in concreto*, means that they are substantial only in conditions which put them beyond all possibility of being, as such, objects of knowledge and experience to radically different ones. We may be to some extent capable of describing such notions as they obtained in former times, so far as evidence remains and we interpret it aright; but the result remains mere description of something that can never become objective and objectified for us in actuality, can never be produced as an object of knowledge and experience, our second Nature and homo faber nature being of so different a kind as to be incapable of accommodating such, to them, wholly alien elements. This does not hold only for homo faber natures now extinct. It does so for contemporaneous ones, so far as these exhibit differences substantial enough to make them in these respects distinct, and the notions corresponding to these unintelligible to one another.

The circumstance explains the unavoidable emptiness of moral or ethical theory which, in wanting to deal with pertinent notions in general, necessarily deprives them of their substance, i.e., of their actuality, as notions given objectivity, objectification only as particular contents determined in terms of the needs of specific homo faber natures to which there accord equally specific second Natures. Moral "laws", like those of dialectics, can never have objective, objectified actuality, any more than can the human nature in general (that taken to be "essential" to "man"), the behaviour of which they prescribe and regulate. They are a sort of semblance, an attempt to give apparently rational form and sanction to that which is but a vain hope grounded in illusion. For such abstractions have in the end always to be imposed, demanding, on the part of those attempting this, the very behaviour the moral law outlaws. Such attempts, that is, of necessity involve self-contradiction.

The unintelligibility of homo faber natures radically different from our own rules out the possibility of there being a human psychology in general that can be produced as an objective, objectified actuality capable of being known and experienced. The idea that certain aspects of human psychology are "innate", belong to "man" as such, any change in which brought about by circumstances being superficial, is no more and can never be more than a groundless supposition, since no possible conditions can be produced which might allow this to be put to the test. What the idea in effect reflects is the fact that our circumstances and our conceptions being what they are and no other, in virtue of the absolute limitation of our perception, knowledge, and experience to just these set by the hypothesis about man and nature of which our society is the expression (and which to us is not a hypothesis but "in the nature of things"), we simply are wholly unable to conceive of a human psychology other than our own, variations granted, in terms of which we needs must (if we wish) represent that of "man" to ourselves. The picture this gives of the past is the more difficult to accept as false, in that it is assumed that because men in the past were, as we now are, engaged in the struggle for survival, the several human psychologies resulting must at bottom be identical, like causes having like effects. This is the more plausible, given that historical reconstruction, the representation of the past as intelligible, necessarily involves the use of what is presently produced as intelligible (other than which nothing is available to us) as the principle in terms of which that reconstruction, that representation, is made. It ensues, then, that, for so long as its process of production be not grasped, history inescapably appears to vindicate the notion of essence, here of the idea that "man", "the struggle for survival," and so forth, have always been fundamentally the same *in concreto*, namely, as they are now (for of nothing else do we have any knowledge and experience), a view which, if consistently held, must also take in the future, and rule out any radical difference prospectively, as it does retrospectively. What results from this, in the form of psychological theories about the nature of "human nature," is plainly semblance, from the several standpoints of which actuality is in the ways corresponding to them, necessarily misconstrued, sc. misconceived and misrepresented.

There is no conflict here with what was said before, that the struggle for survival is a fatality; and that its mode, the production and reproduction of second Nature and simultaneous self-production and self-reproduction of homo faber nature (consequent always upon an initial spontaneous creation, so far as anything radically new comes into being at any time), gives all its effects certain characteristics deriving from production, from the struggle for survival, as such. This bare theoretical and abstract showing of how actuality must, if at all, come about, owing to the nature of production as such, tells us nothing whatever of how it is constituted and established in reality, of what second Nature and homo faber nature consist in, determined at any time and place also by the vicissitudes of circumstances to have actuality as, and in these and these, specific forms and contents. That is to say, the fact that all homo faber natures are products and have necessarily thus characteristics intrinsic to this, has reference to them in the theoretical context of production as such, i.e., considered as its effects. It has none whatever to them as they exist as objective, objectified actualities, as the embodiment of specific features deriving from accidental historical circumstances, in terms of which their capacities and properties are determined *in concreto*. So that the fact that all homo faber natures are as such intelligible in their nature of products, i.e., that the *modus operandi* of their production is, in theory, intelligible in terms of the nature of production as such, in no way alters the fact that as objective, objectified actualities, as those of beings with defined (and limited) needs and capacities in terms of which their several natures are articulated and severally expressive of specific conceptions of human nature (and the second Nature complementing them), they are unintelligible to one another.

A homo faber nature, an expression of production, is structured in terms of the capacities and properties (physical and mental) that have been made actual in it and for it, as objective, objectified features of a second Nature and, as such and as such alone, the warrant of the actuality of that nature which comes to perceive, know, and experience itself only reflexively. It is in this perception, knowledge, and experience of being not merely something determinate but something of determinate use that the possibility of individuality consists at bottom for homo faber. Such determinateness is *eo ipso* the ground for those notions that form an integral part of the expression, the manifestation, of what to this particular homo faber nature is not only its self, but itself *qua* person, however much coloured by the effect of accidental circumstances, fashion, for example.

The idea of individuality as free and unique is self-contradiction. Only what is (to us) spontaneously arisen appears free and unique, and so appearing can be neither known nor experienced for what it really is. It is only when whatever it may be that has so come about initially has been produced, correctly cognised in this context, and become capable of being re-produced, given, that is, objectivity and objectification as a determinate and determined thing in actuality, that it can be re-cognised, perceived, known, and experienced for what it is, a classic, standardised instance, or member of a class, as other than which it can be neither produced nor re-produced, nor, *a fortiori*, be perceived, known, and experienced. Individuality, being what it is as a result of the abstraction and objectification of what have become capacities and properties of some homo faber nature is by that very fact classic, standard. It is, that is, itself typical, any appearance of its not being so being the effect of the accidental circumstances mentioned. The variety of possible individualities, i.e., of the types, derives from the division and specialisation of labour, from the manifold of distinct capacities and properties produced in the course of, and so intrinsic features of, the growth and diversification of production.

So far from being free, individuality is, and can be no other than, an expression of the servitude intrinsic to production. It is a manifestation of homo faber as agent, as means of production simply, as that objective, objectified, sc. actual, capacity and property pertinent to the production of a determined and determinate something (be it what it may) which as end to be achieved itself gives the guiding rule necessary thereto, the *modus operandi*, of which the capacity and property in question are features. That a man may be more than this, his homo faber individuality, is, as already shown, irrelevant to production, and, should this detract from the purity of that individuality, i.e., from that capacity and property in productive employment, an obstacle to production to the extent that it does so, and to be removed, suffer the man what he may. Individuality is *sui generis* a manifestation of the deformation consequent upon the specialisation and division of labour, but for which production, other than the crudest, would be impossible. As such a manifestation, individuality betrays the aggression and violence unavoidable to its constitution, in that it can be what it is only as a result in the first instance of the abstraction, the appropriation, of that which, as subsequently produced, becomes its capacity, its property, in terms of which it manifests itself. In this very abtraction, or appropriation, is contained the injustice inherent in production, the very establishment of a capacity, a property, involving one-sidedness, as the negation of that which, in terms of the very determination of a capacity, a property, becomes unknowable, though nonetheless real. Individuality is the mark of the fact that integrity, wholeness (however it be thought of) is by definition impossible to homo faber, whether he be by force of circumstances the manifestation of some one capacity or property, or of several, since its very expression in terms of a capacity, a property (but for which it could not be) is the index of the violence done to a (wholly abstractly conceivable) whole, and sign of its destruction. The idea of what constitutes a well-rounded individuality thus inevitably involves some dogmatic presupposition (at bottom about the "nature" of man) that limits the possibilities to those which are acceptable in terms of that idea, of the particular point of view that it expresses. An example is the Greek view of professional skill as banausic, undignified, consequent upon a specific idea of what is proper to a "free" man.

One effect of modern technology is the greater simplification and standardisation of many of the operations still to be carried out by labour and, therefore, of the capacities and properties required to that end. The very division and specialisation of labour which once resulted in the possibility of more diverse individualities, today in many instances so reduces the capacities and properties required in production from human labour, and by that so standardises them further, that the individuality that remains possible in terms of these shows itself plainly in actuality as what it inherently is, typical and classic, one that, relative to the persons involved, is in other than the general respect that determines the type or class, quite indeterminate, namely, standard and unindividual. The desire so often voiced today to be "different" without further specification, as if "difference" were an actual, determinate something in itself that one could be in reality, that would give one some specific individuality peculiar to oneself, is a reflection of this. It exhibits itself in practice most often as quirkiness, oddity in bearing, dress, speech, taste, and so forth, unrelated to anything other than the wish to assert a difference, i.e., to assert an individuality, as if it could, in the form of this sham external, become that of which production itself deprives it.

With every removal from homo faber of a capacity, a property, by technology, there is removed as well the individuality (or aspect of it) corresponding thereto, and its very possibility. Where this removal is accompanied by the creation and production of a new capacity, new property, that loss is compensated for by the gain of the possibility of some new expression of individuality (or aspect of it). This is not to say that the person for whom the possibility of individuality has wholly or partly disappeared with the obsolescence of the production and related property, capacity, that gave rise to it, is necessarily the one who is compensated for this by the gain of the new. It is to say no more than that, society taken as a whole, the loss can, and may well be, compensated for by a gain, i.e., someone can, and may, gain a new possibility. But that is in no way necessary. There may simply be a loss.

Such a loss, should it occur, does not dispose of the aggression, the violence, inseparable from the formation of individuality. It is a loss simply of a means of its productive employment, of its constructive expression. The aggression, the violence, remains, and, should no new possibility of

100

its productive employment come about, without any but destructive outlet. Other possibilities wanting, it can even become itself the capacity, the property, in terms of which some sort of individuality can assert itself, aggressive, violent behaviour as such, becoming then the appropriate manner of its manifestation, and a need demanding satisfaction. Where this is so, where aggression, violence, has itself become the principle of individuation, it no longer requires any object other than itself. Its purpose, that of expressing and manifesting individuality, fulfils itself in the very commission of aggression, of violence, to which its, so to say material, becomes something wholly indifferent. It is not in appearance only that such aggression, such violence, of its very nature indiscriminate, is mindless. Every loss of capacity, of property, is a loss of the objectivity, the objectification in terms of which second Nature is constituted as capable of being perceived, known, and experienced as rational, and therewith, reflexively, homo faber nature as likewise to that extent rational. The loss of individuality, in part or in whole, is inescapably in that measure a loss of rationality, something tending to be more evident in immature persons, in that rationality (so far as accords with some capacities, some properties become objective and objectified) has not become to that extent established and habitual, and capable of persisting to some extent, despite the loss of the capacities, the properties, themselves in question.

But these are general considerations that flow from the fact that homo faber nature as such is produced and has certain characteristics intrinsic to it *qua* product. They tell one nothing about how homo faber nature expresses itself *in concreto*, in the determinate content and form given it by accidental historical circumstances at any time and place. With homo faber natures radically different from our own, it is pointless to concern ourselves, since they are all *a priori* unintelligible to us. But just here, with respect to ourselves, to present homo faber nature that would seem, if at all, knowable, just here is it that the notion of excess fundamental to an understanding of what homo faber nature must be in its present incarnation, reveals itself most clearly to be that which makes it altogether impossible to represent this nature to ourselves as other than semblance. For, owing to the limits of the possibility of perception, knowledge, and experience set by society as the expression of the exhaustive hypothesis concerning nature and man now ruling, there can be no reference to something other than this that might provide the ground necessary to the determination of what this excess consists in, i.e., might exhibit it to us not only as what it actually is, but also as, of its very nature, hypothetical. The semblance here consists in our having to take this hypothesis about the nature of homo faber that is ours as if it were so "by nature," i.e., were as such the nature of "man" (and likewise the second Nature that accords with it, the nature of "nature in itself"). Even retrospectively, it is impossible, with any certainty, to know a previous homo faber nature in terms of the excess intrinsic to it, since what we believe ourselves to perceive

101

as excess in it is something that derives from our own radically different homo faber nature as yardstick, the very factor that absolutely removes that previous one from all possibility of being perceived, known, and experienced in its own terms. The excess that we imagine ourselves to perceive in our own homo faber nature is of a wholly different kind from that so far discussed, as will be evident from the following.

Marx's comment that technology is the open revelation of human faculties, i.e., capacities, properties, is an adequate starting point, provided this be understood as referring to homo faber strictly, and even so, that the properties in question, the capacities, are not all there is to homo faber, who must be presumed to be capable of alteration in ways presently unforeseeable and unknowable to us. Technology is not just the revelation of the capacities, the properties of homo faber. It is at the same time that of the needs of homo faber directly and indirectly associated with them. These together are not to be taken to be an effect of homo faber nature. They are themselves, as objective and objectified actualities, that homo faber nature as so produced, and warrant of its actuality. The revelation of homo faber capacities, properties, relating to technology is inseparable from the simultaneous revelation of the associated capacities, properties, of the material needed for that technology, i.e., of that second Nature that is an integral part of that homo faber nature as that but for which the said capacities and properties could not have arisen and become capable of being produced, of becoming means of production (and vice versa). What this technology, i.e., this second Nature and homo faber nature, is in actuality, nowise (as earlier argued) necessarily exhausts what it could in principle be. It is what the accidental historical circumstances in which this takes place have determined it to be, circumstances which, however much they bear the impress of production as it is at any time, are themselves never, and never can be, wholly determined by it, or they could not be what they are, accidental and historical, for all that they owe the former in some measure to production itself, to the extent that they are the effect of its intrinsic, internal accidentality. The determination in question self-evidently cannot be in terms of those needs that derive from production in the narrow technical sense of that term, but in that of others produced in terms of these very accidental circumstances that give the struggle for survival its form and content *in concreto*, that of a specific society that is the expression of some exhaustive hypothesis about the nature of second Nature and man, that sets the limits to the possibility of perception, knowledge, and experience, i.e., absolutely rules out any not in terms set by itself.

The question of how such a hypothesis itself originally arises is rationally unanswerable, since, as at first radically new, it can have come about only spontaneously, i.e., in a manner unknowable to us. It is only as having become conventional that its effects can become objects for, and of, perception, knowledge, and experience. When that occurs, it is a sign that enough of the new this allows of has become capable of being produced and re-produced, has been given the needed actuality as determinate and determined causal processes yielding determined and determinate effects; and therewith the homo faber nature equipped with the relevant perception, knowledge, and experience, of which what has been made actual then appears as the open revelation and witness to its actuality. What is actual, however, is of course not for the perception, knowledge, and experience for which it is so, hypothetical. That is to say, the very circumstance that a hypothesis about a second Nature and accordant homo faber nature has become conventional, that second Nature and homo faber nature have been produced and re-produced as its expression in actuality, such that perception, knowledge, and experience are what they are only as informed by it, that very circumstance is the ground of its disappearance as a hypothesis, i.e., of its never being capable of being perceived, known, and experienced for what it is, a hypothesis merely; but of its necessarily being taken to be "in the nature of things," such that a nature in any way radically different from it becomes altogether inconceivable, as does a human nature. Yet without a knowledge of how such a hypothesis arises, it becomes impossible to establish precisely when it did so. The several incompatible views about when to date the origin of present (capitalist) society is witness to this, to the fact that there is no one circumstance or set of circumstances so self-evidently decisive as to be generally acceptable as constituting the criterion that would allow some date, or fairly narrow range of dates, to be agreed upon as definitive. The difficulty cannot be resolved, since, once a hypothesis has established itself, i.e., once a society has come to be constituted in terms of it, its manifestations become so varied and at the same time so indissolubly interconnected at any time that it becomes impossible to determine any order of priority among them, other than in terms of some dogmatic presupposition, some presupposition itself not susceptible of being put to the test. The history that is constructed in such terms (whatever they may be) can be but semblance, among the various forms of which no rational choice is possible.

The sum of all capacities, properties, and needs, those that have been created and reproduced as part of production in the narrow sense, as well as those that have been created and reproduced as part of the accidental historical circumstances in which the struggle for survival takes place, is what at any time constitutes homo faber nature, and exists in the abstracted and objectified (reified and alienated) form of objects that witnesses to its being what it is in actuality. The more varied the capacities, properties, and needs created and reproduced, the more varied the homo faber nature, the less does it become possible for any one person to perceive, know, and experience it as a whole, i.e., to be the manifestation of that homo faber nature in its entirety.

Of this comprehensive homo faber nature, individual persons have that part that falls to their lot as determined by accidental circumstances of birth, milieu, education, wealth, intelligence, and so forth. These individual natures are then constituted by selection of some from among the sum of possibilities contained in homo faber nature as a whole, and so far as they differ from one another (more as types than as single natures), have standpoints in these respects peculiar to themselves which determine how they perceive, know, and experience the world (including homo faber nature), both of which tend to be rational to them only within the limits set by these standpoints, i.e., by the properties and capacities which their homo faber nature manifests, having been determined and constituted by them to be so. They, of course, all have in common those basic characteristics referred to deriving from the fact that homo faber nature has been produced as part of the struggle for survival. But the form in which they manifest themselves is determined not by this (which simply necessitates their arising) but by the accidental historical circumstances in which the struggle for survival and the production therewith associated takes place. It is in terms of these circumstances that hierarchies of needs come to be established together with the order of priority of their satisfaction, i.e., that from among the possibilities in principle available to production at whatever stage, some and not others are chosen and become actual not just in general, but, barring accidents, specifically in such quantity and quality as accords with the given hierarchy. The homo faber natures so constituted are the only ones available to perception, knowledge, and experience. It is in terms of them that ideas about "human nature" (as such) are formed, relative to some conception, inevitably dogmatic, and, rational as it may seem, but semblance, of the purpose of human existence (and therewith of that of "Nature") which decides what shall be considered proper to "human nature," what capacities, properties, needs, shall be taken in relation to it to be natural, what unnatural, what artificial and so on.

It is from such dogmatic conceptions of "human nature" that the idea of what appears "excess" is derived, one that clearly is very different from that earlier discussed. For in this form, it is (whatever may be fancied by those who take it to be "true") always evidence of prejudice, for it arises not merely from the inability to perceive, know, and experience the world as other than the limitations of some particular type of homo faber human nature has determined it, but from the inability, often unwillingness, to concede that there may be other worlds, other needs, capacities, and properties, that "human nature" may be more and other than the one that passes judgment. Such a judgment can, of course, also be made by one homo faber nature of another similarly constituted, owing to greed, envy, malice, hatred, and so on (characteristics *in abstracto* of all homo faber natures, however differently constituted, that are inevitable accompaniments of competition, aggression, i.e., of the struggle for survival).

In accord with the idea of homo faber nature, of its being, together with the society and second Nature of which it is a part, merely a hypothesis about the nature of man which has changed radically from time to time, the term "human nature," as referring to a constant that could be produced, given objective, objectified actuality, is devoid of meaning, since this production is impossible. In this context "human nature" is a conception necessarily deriving from actual homo faber nature (other than which none exists) and being so, can have reference to no other radically different homo faber nature, the radical difference of which from the one actually existing removing it from all possibility of being perceived, known, and experienced as and for what it was when actually existing (or will be, if the future is in question). "Human nature" is unavoidably a historical construct and as such a reconstruction of the past in terms of the present that of its very nature is beyond proof or disproof (and similarly of the future). It is, in short, semblance and can never be anything else, any more than can the study of it, however in appearance scientifically undertaken. However, even supposing this not to be so, even supposing it were possible to produce a homo faber nature that was, so to say, the essence of all possible such natures, and give it objective, objectified actuality, so that scientific knowledge of it became possible, even so, this would still yield no knowledge of "human nature" which, in the very terms of the idea of homo faber nature as inherently partial, one-sided, would still be more and other than this. And this "more" that is human nature as it is beyond production and everything it gives rise to, would be by this very circumstance beyond the possibility of being perceived, known, and experienced, perception, knowledge, and experience as known to us being what they are owing to their having been part of production, as having been produced as capacities and properties of homo faber.

In reality, however, we have not to do with this, but with conceptions of "human nature" that result from specialisation and division of labour, such as they manifest themselves as determined by present accidental historical circumstances. These, as just argued, are of their very nature partial and one-sided in that what is chosen as the decisive, determining factor must needs be seen to be so from the limited standpoint of some particular type of homo faber nature which is then unavoidably made into the exemplar of homo faber natures in that basic respect, sc. of "human nature" (there being for the conceptions in question no idea of homo faber nature). The dogmatic nature of such a standpoint makes it inescapably sectarian and polemical in relation to all other equally dogmatic and sectarian standpoints likewise at war with one another. The differences among these, all forms of semblance, are not resolvable by appeal to evidence, since what evidence there is for each has been produced by each in terms of the very dogmatic presuppositions to be put to the test, any phenomena adduced by rival dogmas in disproof inevitably being dismissed as tendentious, as indeed they are.

Were the argument to be continued beyond this point, it would become even more repetitious than it has, so far, necessarily been. It would manifest the closed circularity of our world in which second nature is what it is in response to the needs of homo faber, the nature of which is what it is owing to the fact that, in the given accidental historical circumstances in which the struggle for survival takes place, second Nature has been created, produced, and re-produced as it has, only as the effect of the capacities and properties of homo faber, itself created, produced, and re-produced to that end. The society these together constitute is thus *sui generis*, a complete, and completely self-enclosed, world, the capacities and properties of which, the open revelation of the nature of "Nature" and of homo faber as thereby constituted and established in actuality, can produce, viz., re-produce, only itself, which to itself needs must then appear "in the nature of things." The failure of all attempts to do other than this, to, with the given capacities and properties alone existing and available, produce a radically different society becomes intelligible as the inevitable result of trying to do the impossible. The following may, all the same, be of help in emphasising the point, and removing whatever illusions remain, with respect to the possibility of envisaging in any way whatever a future radically different from the present, for better or worse.

VII

Such a (better) world—the worse is of no concern here—is commonly thought of as one in which peace, freedom, and plenty have been achieved. Freedom left aside, the question arises how the remaining two are at all to be reconciled, when the production of the one rules out the other.

There is no call here to repeat the arguments showing that production, need, and the accordant capacities and properties involve competition, aggression, violence (injustice, wrong) in some form, and that homo faber nature is thus necessarily also competitive, aggressive, and unjust, however this be qualified in actuality, held in check to some extent by some social mechanism. Intrinsic to production is accidentality (internal and external) which in some measure constantly upsets the social equilibrium (so far as there can be said to be one) resulting from the regulation of existing production, existing opportunities for competition, aggression, violence, i.e., from the determination of the extent to which the exploitation of productive techniques shall be allowed, since this accidentality results in new techniques and new possibilities of exploitation, new means of competition, aggression, violence, to which the regulations in force do not necessarily apply. Production indeed can become so varied and its accidentality so considerable, that such regulations become ever more difficult to achieve, especially when to the accidentality directly arising from production, there be added that deriving from historical circumstances—circumstances which, though they themselves have not been produced, or been produced only in part, nonetheless determine what of the possibilities in principle open to production shall become actual, and the manner in which it shall be done. Accidentality itself is, moreover, a mode of violence, its coming-to-be necessarily in some fashion an eruption into, and disruption of, "normality" (conditions brought about under the guidance of productive rule), there being no possibility of foreknowing where, when, and how what comes about in such fashion will do so, and therefore no possibility of so arranging matters as to minimise, if not wholly to prevent, its disruptive effects, in the given circumstances.

That there can exist circumstances in which some degree of control is possible seems to be suggested by the existence for comparatively long periods of the "cold societies." These, however, were sheltered societies. What impinged upon them in normal conditions was what occurred in the neighbourhood which, at its most extensive, could not comprise a large area. The relative equilibrium they appear to have achieved was not, and could not be, proof against radical alteration of the neighbourhood, direct or indirect, which produced forces and movements wholly beyond their capacity for adjustment.

The achievement of some kind of equilibrium is thus not merely a question of determining what quantum of production will bring this about, what the environment can sustain without gross injury. As determining a factor is the reduction of the accidentality of historical circumstances, the possibility of which, it seems to me indisputable, will be inversely related to the size of the neighbourhood, which thus becomes a factor of crucial importance.

Nowadays, with modern communications, the neighbourhood is the world, and the extent of historical accidentality that affects societies is immeasurably greater. This aspect of the achievement of equilibrium (always relative, of course) involves purely practical questions wholly impossible to frame, let alone to solve, in advance of the establishment of the conditions that would enable the nature of the problems raised by this requirement to be correctly apprehended, and so amenable to resolution. In what follows, I therefore deal only with production in its relation to the possible establishment of an equilibrium of some sort.

(Mention ought to be made here, as much in relation to the "cold societies" as to all others, including our own, of possible perturbations arising in first Nature and in any remaining original, which might conceivably affect second Nature in any way. These, of course, as is clear from the distinctions I have, I hope clearly, made, are altogether beyond any possibility of being perceived, known, and experienced for what they actually may be; so that it becomes pointless to discuss them in relation to any attempt to achieve some sort of equilibrium, or better, some sort of relative stasis.)

Homo faber nature alters with every alteration in production, since no such change is possible without the creation, production, and reproduction of the appropriate new capacities and properties in material and agent, and therewith, new needs requiring to be met as part of that altered nature, a requirement essential to its expression as that nature in actuality. If it be supposed that these new needs are an addition to those already existing, the greater variety and multiplicity of needs resulting signalises an increase in the possibilities for competition, aggression, and violence in the world (second Nature and homo faber nature) produced in terms of them.

Plenty is no abstraction, but a condition the idea of which is necessarily represented in terms of what actually is taken to constitute it, i.e., of what a person would have today, were he living in what is considered to be that condition. Given the existence of different types of homo faber nature as an unavoidable consequence of the manifold variety of produced capacities and properties and accordant needs, together with the possibility of their satisfaction, in existence today, it is plain that each such type will tend to represent the notion of plenty to itself in the, in some fashion idealised, terms of its own nature and needs. That is to say, exceptions granted, every such idea will be the expression of a determination arrived at from a more or less partisan standpoint not only of what is necessary to the very idea of plenty, but also of what is not necessary to it. These various ideas of plenty are, of course, not static. They alter with changes in production, in concomitant capacities, properties, and needs, such that not only can yesterday's luxury become today's necessity, but wholly new products can come about and be taken to be elements essential to the very notion of plenty. It goes without saying that general agreement about what constitutes plenty is unlikely ever to be reached. Or, put differently, it is evident that the only general agreement possible would have to take the form of the sum of all such varying plenties, would necessarily be nothing but an idealised version of existing society. This idealisation dismissed as fanciful illusion, only existing society remains. This indeed can be the only possible result of the attempt to represent the idea of plenty in concrete terms, since, as already remarked, existing society is itself the expression of homo faber nature as a whole in actuality, and the manifestation not merely of its needs, but the expression also of their satisfaction. This is quite other than the satisfaction of the needs of the several types of homo faber nature taken specifically, something decided not by what may be available for the purpose *in abstracto*, but by what the given accidental historical circumstances determine there to be available for each particular purpose in actuality, i.e., for each particular nature. The association of peace with such a representation, in part or in sum the only possible one if it be desired to give the abstraction "plenty" some embodiment, some appearance of possible actuality, is a manifest absurdity. This is so with reference not merely to external conditions. It is so also with reference to those internal to homo faber himself, his psychological state, caught up as he is in the struggle for survival, the goal of which for each type is, in principle or in actuality to a greater or lesser extent (something decided by circumstances), the nearest approximation to the plenty it represents to itself as the ideal condition of life (exceptions once more granted).

It follows that if there were ever to be a future in which (so far as is consonant with the yet to some indeterminate extent remaining struggle for survival) men were at peace with one another and (necessary complement) with themselves, it would have to be of a nature radically different from the present. Such difference would not just affect this or that particular aspect of society, of second Nature and homo faber nature; but would bespeak their thoroughgoing alteration. Some of these differences can be hinted at by inference, hints which, bare as they needs must be, suffice to show why a world, an existence, of that kind must be inconceivable to us.

What follows has as its premise the nature of homo faber and second Nature as they actually exist at present. For all that it is plain that great changes are in the offing, given the possibilities, however remote still in appearance, opened up by technology—changes that in all likelihood will make this last section, or part of it, incorrect and irrelevant; for all that, to speculate about the matter would be not just vain; it would far more importantly mean the surrender of the critical standpoint so far (I believe) held to. What the future holds, the future will disclose. Reason, however, can and must attend only to what at any moment is actual, to what exists as an objective, objectified part of the produced (objective and objectified) world, as at that moment it is, namely, to the given second Nature and complementary homo faber nature.

These alone taken into account, what at the moment presents itself as one of the prime requirements of that mentioned radically different world seems to be the reduction not just of the competition, aggression, violence, accidentality of the produced world (that includes homo faber nature), but of their very possibility, in effect, the reduction of production. In practice, however, the matter looks considerably different. It is not simply the quantity of objects produced, the reduction of which is in question, but their kinds. This, if it involves the loss of some possibilities of competition, aggression, etc., at the same time involves the loss of capacities, properties, and needs of material and agent that are the effect of these. As objective, objectified actualities, they are not just aspects of homo faber nature as a whole and taken to be so by one or other type of homo faber nature in which they feature. They appear to these types to be essential elements of the plenty that is to them their ideal condition, i.e., of what is proper to the "nature of man." The needed reduction in the possibility of competition, aggression, violence, and accidentality in effect not only bespeaks what, in terms of present homo faber nature, both appears and actually is an empoverishment, but to those homo faber natures for which what is to be lost appears essential to their very being, to go against "human nature" (as indeed in the given terms it does). It goes quite against Utopian fantasies of "the development of the free human personality" as many-sided and infinitely varied, that takes as given the possibilities actually available in existing second Nature and homo faber nature as a result of existing production and available only in existing conditions, i.e., with the drawbacks attendant upon this. Such fancy, however, supposes it to be somehow possible to have the good without the evil inseparable from it, and so doing condemns itself as vain. The very concept of Utopia, moreover, even in its most appealing, aesthetic, guise, goes against what Western tradition has understandably determined to be, in whatever form this may be, the Good.

The struggle for survival, the form of which is production, puts a premium on activity. In the nature of finite teleology, the activity in question is that of the telos that determines and directs material and agent, i.e., imparts to them the movement (activity) proper to them in relation to itself as the purpose to be achieved. In a world conceived on this pattern, activity necessarily appears the ruling, formative, principle, but for which that which becomes material and agent would remain inert and shapeless, lacking all capacities and properties other than these. The translation of such a conception into more abstract religious (theological) and philosophical terms (as God, Soul, Light, Power, Mind, and so forth) is virtually a matter of course, so soon as cognition has become capable of such general reflection, viz., as enough of the world has been created, produced, and re-produced to enable reflection of the required generality to take place.

Without going further into this here, it is plain that of the Good conceived after the model of finite teleology, activity must be an essential attribute, something which is so part of Western thought that it can only with difficulty (if at all) accommodate the idea of "inactivity" as a good. Sloth is one of the deadly sins, and the terms available for the description of "inactivity" (other than in its approved form of a rest from exertion, in order the better to be active thereafter) are almost all pejorative: laziness, idleness, stagnation, etc. But activity in the context of finite teleology is purposive activity, in that its intrinsic intention is to impose its own will upon what to it, whether material or agent, is to be simply means to an end of its own, i.e., to determine that means as this and nothing else, and compel it to abide by this determination until the end has been effected, be the result for the means as other than this what it may, or its suffering, as so reduced to nothing but means. In a world of purposes to be realised, peace in its proper signification has no place. And this is so not just of second Nature and homo faber nature in relation to it as its producer, but also of homo faber in relation to himself as self-producer. Whatever appears as peace, if any such appearance there be, can be only the result of domination, of the repression of what goes against the purpose (or purposes) to be realised. In the given context, it is both violence and violation, even if in covert form. And however better it may be than overt violence and violation, this remains its nature nonetheless, as any serious attempt to resist will quickly show.

A world in which, relative to second Nature, there is less possibility of aggression, violence, competition, is one in which the parallel lessening of the possibility of these relative to homo faber nature must also be accompanied by a lessening of activity.

The check comes here. The attempt to represent what this lessening of activity might involve elucidates the fact that no terms are available that

111

do not derive from the world constituted by, and as the effect of, purposive activity, production. Even to describe this as a lessening of activity is to do so from the standpoint of this activity. And yet what it is, other than this, is beyond conception. It is not leisure, which is a category of production, of the activity required by it, a need of homo faber as agent. This lessening of activity which involves a shrinkage of homo faber nature *pari passu* with that of second Nature (necessarily, they being one) betokens that what this leaves behind is something other than second Nature and homo faber nature, of which no conception, perception, experience is possible to any homo faber nature caught up, and formed, in the struggle for survival. Aside perhaps from the wrestlings of Plotinus with the intractable difficulty of showing that what from the standpoint of the struggle for survival appears to be a total absence of activity is not on that account to be taken simply as nothingness, the conceptions formed of this absence, all necessarily deriving from the struggle for survival, from production, productive activity, are precisely of that kind. Indeed, so impossible is it to conceive of this absence as other than a negation, a privation, that even where, as in some Eastern beliefs, such activity is itself taken to be, though essential and unavoidable, an evil, the beatific state that is the goal of existence and comes about only with the cessation of activity in all its conceivable forms (internal and external) is seen as a complete vanishing, as utter nothingness, as death for the individuals achieving this culmination of perfection.

The question whether such a condition, that would not be nothingness, or death, in the conventional sense alone available to us at present, be possible is one we cannot answer, any more than the question whether if it be it is that in which freedom (in Kant's sense) is to be found, though, as I have already argued, I presume that this would be so. What is certain is that peace, which (other than as wholly negative, as a mere temporary absence of activity) has a relation of mutual exclusion to the struggle for survival, will be found here, if at all. What it is, however, cannot be described. The attempt to do so in aesthetic terms is, as said, self-defeating, since the very terms that must be used (individuality, self-consciousness, moral perfection, and so on) belong wholly to homo faber nature.

A warning is in place here. It is a mistake to suppose that though "Nature" is pregnant with as yet unrealised possibilities, man is excluded from this; namely, to take for granted that the human capacities so far produced constitute the full extent of what is available to man. Nothing supports, or can support, this belief which rests on a failure to grasp to its fullest extent, and accept, one of the very few things that history, despite its ineradically tendentious nature, makes plain: that is, that the future always has surprises which make it different from whatever has been expected as what it will be. There is no reason to suppose that until such time as it vanishes (at least in any of the forms presently known to us) life (to restrict myself to this here) will not continue to manifest radical changes that overset what may seem at any time to be its culminating and ultimate achievements. Thus to dismiss the idea that there is something beyond second Nature and homo faber nature, beyond necessity, as mystical nonsense, simply because what this is cannot be brought within the compass of reason as we presently know it, is nothing but dogmatism arrogantly assuming that what it fancies itself to know is all that can rationally be known.

So far as the ideal of a "planned society" is concerned, with which peace, plenty, freedom are normally unthinkingly associated, this much may be said. The very circumstance that accidentality is inherent in production (as both internal and external) means that planning, namely control, of production as a whole is the more impossible, the more diversified and extensive it is. The reduction of competition, violence, and aggression discussed above will, it is to be presumed, be accompanied by a reduction in the accidentality it generates; and this is as far as control can actually go, since there are no possible circumstances in which, given any production at all, accidentality does not arise, any more than competition, aggression, and violence (injustice). Everything said in this essay makes it plain that a shrinkage of homo faber nature and second Nature necessarily involves a shrinkage of society, of the organised (servile) activity in terms of which the struggle for survival is carried on. And just as what lies beyond homo faber nature and second Nature is inconceivable to us, so *a fortiori* is that which lies beyond society.

That brings me to the final point: the impossibility of conceiving how such a radically different future could come about which, so far as present homo faber can possibly (mis)represent it to himself, i.e., in terms of existing society, must appear a return to a wholly unacceptable poverty and primitiveness, wholly impossible, other than under strongest duress.

It is self-evident that such a future could, if at all, be achieved, once its initial spontaneous coming-to-be had taken place, only after much trial and error, experiment, in the course of which a new human nature would come into being of which homo faber nature could be only a subordinate part, and with it a world of which second Nature in whatever form produced would likewise be only a part, a travail during which natures incapable of adaptation to the radically new would die out. It would, to begin with, be a forty years in the wilderness. However, whether this can be, and how, are matters not susceptible even of discussion, a human nature, and Nature, that have not been produced, being something altogether beyond the bounds of possibility, at least to conception.

Nonetheless, it is impossible legitimately to predetermine whether freedom and peace (other than as the qualified servitude and absence of overt conflict alone possible today) must remain nothing but an idea. To suppose so means to go beyond the bounds of knowledge, however much it may appear that this must be so in terms of what it is possible for homo faber nature to represent to itself as actual, as capable of being given effect.

Nothing written in this essay is put forward with any claim to finality. What is put forward is offered simply as a tool, by the use of which better results may be obtained than have been with tools now in use, until such time as, it is to be hoped, a yet more useful one shall have been devised.

That, contrasted with the consolations of Utopia, the result reached here is on any conventional showing bleak must be admitted. But Utopia is illusion, the attempt to have the good of the produced world in all its extension and variety, without its inseparably attendant evil.

From the standpoint of critique, matters look different. From here the future would be bleak indeed, if nothing were available other than what is known and knowable, if, that is, all that were available fell within the compass of homo faber nature and second Nature, of production. For then, whatever might come to pass would be nothing but a variation on a theme the nature of which has been the subject of this essay. Just this, however, the very conception of homo faber and second Nature shows to be a theoretically unwarranted extension. The critique of production concludes in the assertion that production can never be other than intrinsically limited, incomplete, that there is more than the actuality to which it gives rise, notwithstanding that in terms of that actuality itself, of that thereby alone made known and knowable (second Nature and homo faber), perception, knowledge, and experience of this more is absolutely impossible.

This conclusion of rational inquiry must needs be optimistic, even if this optimism be necessarily a matter of faith. It is the optimism that arises from the realisation that the world need not be some form of that which it is now, but can be fundamentally other than this. This must encourage hope and enable a nature strong enough to bear the loss of illusion to face present and future ills with greater fortitude and serenity, buoyed up by the conviction that the full story has not been told, that there are more things in heaven and earth than are dreamt of in philosophy.

But that is as it may be. To have removed some illusions about the nature of freedom and peace, and their relation to what is necessarily involved by, and in, the struggle for survival, by, and in, production; to have shown that there is, in the very nature of production, more to man and Nature than their produced forms of homo faber and second Nature; and, in the process, to have redefined the boundaries of knowledge, and distinguished it from semblance, while acknowledging that semblance is an unavoidable, indeed, a perhaps necessary, feature of human life as we know it—to have done this (supposing it to have been done, as I do), is, all qualifications granted, nonetheless an achievement of some value.